Be Still

A PREGNANCY BED REST DEVOTIONAL

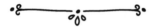

Stacey Pylman

WESTBOW
PRESS®
A DIVISION OF THOMAS NELSON
& ZONDERVAN

WestBow Press books may be ordered through booksellers or by contacting:

WestBow Press
A Division of Thomas Nelson & Zondervan
1663 Liberty Drive
Bloomington, IN 47403
www.westbowpress.com
844-714-3454

Interior Image Credit: Natalie Jelsema

ISBN: 978-1-6642-6818-0 (sc)
ISBN: 978-1-6642-6819-7 (hc)
ISBN: 978-1-6642-6817-3 (e)

Library of Congress Control Number: 2022910637

Print information available on the last page.

WestBow Press rev. date: 06/29/2022

Dedication

I dedicate this devotional to my three wonderful daughters. You are extraordinary gifts from God. I am so glad He chose me to be your mom. Someday you will face challenges that will feel impossible to overcome, but if you look at the very beginning of your lives, before you were even born, you can see that God has always had a perfect plan for you, and He will carry you through.

With Love,
Mom

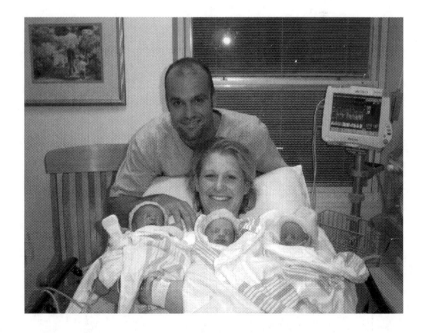

Contents

A Note from the Author

I lived in the hospital for eight weeks on bed rest before giving birth to my triplet girls in 2006. The days were long and often very uncomfortable. I was plagued by worries and just plain tired. What got me through was my faith in God.

Living on bed rest was a very hard, soul-searching, and remarkable time in my life. I started having contractions while twenty-six weeks pregnant with triplets. I went to the emergency room, not knowing it would become my new home for untold weeks. Even after I was admitted, I thought they would get my contractions under control, and I would leave again. However, the doctors felt it was best that I stay under their watchful eyes. I knew it was the best place for me, but I never thought I could do bed rest for that long. What I didn't realize was that I wasn't going to do it; God was. It was my faith in God and His care that brought me through the challenges of bed rest. He cared for me through my nurses, doctors, visitors, family, and friends. The verses my friends and family shared with me during bed rest became very cherished words that helped me through the tough days ahead.

Years after my girls were born, God put the desire on my heart to write a devotional for women on bed rest. I wanted to share with these brave women encouragement from the scripture, words of comfort from someone who had been there, and the love of Jesus. I slowly began writing devotionals when my daughters were three years old. Obviously, carving out time to write with young triplets was difficult. When my daughters reached kindergarten, I decided to go back to school. School and work slowed me down even more. Yet God still had plans for this devotional. So many women were going to be on bed rest who needed to hear words of comfort from their God. It is when we or our children are helpless, vulnerable, and scared that we find the most comfort from God— that is, if we let Him. Again, God put the desire on my heart to continue writing.

I pray you are blessed by the words of encouragement found in this devotional. I hope the Bible verses, my stories, the songs, and my bed rest survival tips provide encouragement for you as you spend your days on bed rest. I leave you with these words:

> God doesn't give us what we can handle;
> God helps us handle what we are given.

You are loved, and you can do this!

—Stacey Pylman, PhD, and mother of wonderful triplet girls

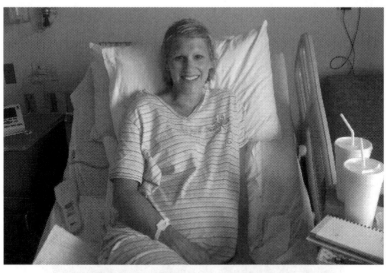

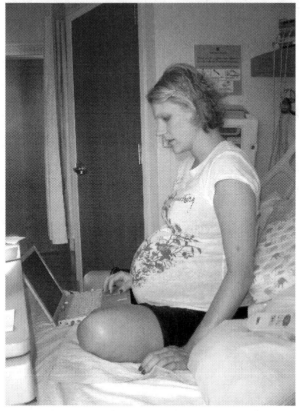

1

This Is a Season, Not Forever

But I trust in you, O Lord; I say "You are my
God." My times are in your hands.

—PSALM 31:14–15

There is a time for everything, and a season
for every activity under the heavens.

—ECCLESIASTES 3:1

So we fix our eyes not on what is seen, but what is unseen,
since what is seen is temporary, but what is unseen is eternal.

—2 CORINTHIANS 4:18

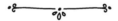

*How will I ever survive being on bed rest? There is no way I will stay
sane lying there day after day!* I thought before being put on bed
rest. When the day finally came, I realized it was something I had
to do for a while. It was for the good of my babies, and I had no
choice. I actually felt safe there because it was safe for the babies.

The key for me was remembering it was only for season—in
my case the summer season. I remember sitting in my hospital

room and watching the summer days slip by one after another. I mourned swimming in the lake, feeling the warmth of the sun on my skin, taking long walks, and celebrating the Fourth of July. I often joked that it was the summer that never was, but I knew I had many more summers ahead of me—summers with my babies.

Many times in life, God asks us to endure hardships for a season. Sometimes it is a season of doing without, sometimes a season of mourning, loneliness, or pain. Whatever the season, God promises these things: He will be there with you during this season, this season will not last forever, and out of this season, He will bring good. This season, your time on bed rest, is in His hands.

L I S T E N

"Every Season" by Nichole Nordeman
"Seasons" by Hillsong Worship

Bed Rest Survival Tip

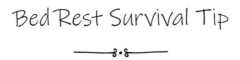

Make a countdown calendar. Nothing feels better than crossing off a day or week. Write your gestational weeks on it and watch your progress. Write down special visits, parties, or events coming up so you have something to focus on and look forward to. Put your due date on the calendar so you can visualize the end goal.

2

The Author and Creator of Life

With the help of the Lord I have brought forth a man.
—GENESIS 4:1

Now the Lord was gracious to Sarah as he had said, and
the Lord did for Sarah what he had promised. Sarah
became pregnant and bore a son to Abraham in his
old age, at the very time God had promised him.
—GENESIS 21:1–2

Then God remembered Rachel; he listened
to her and enabled her to conceive.
—GENESIS 30:22

For you created my inmost being; you knit me together in
my mother's womb. I praise you because I am fearfully and
wonderfully made; your works are wonderful, I know that full
well. My frame was not hidden from you when I was made in
the secret place, when I was woven together in the depths of the
earth. Your eyes saw my unformed body; all the days ordained
for me were written in your book before one of them came to be.
—PSALM 139:13–16

After this his wife Elizabeth became pregnant ... "The Lord has done this for me," she said. "In these days he has shown his favor and taken away my disgrace among the people."

—LUKE 1:24–25

Every good and perfect gift is from above, coming down from the Father of heavenly lights, who does not change like shifting shadows. He chose to give us birth through the word of truth, that we might be a kind of first-fruits of all he created.

—JAMES 1:17–18

The Bible is very clear that God is in charge of conception. He decides when to bring new life into the world, and He doesn't stop at conception. He continues to form the baby cell by cell into a beautiful masterpiece.

The narration at the beginning of Sandi Patty's song "Masterpiece," taken from Psalm 139:13–16, describes God's work so well. "You made my whole being. You formed me in my mother's body. You saw my bones being formed as I took shape in my mother's body. When I was put together there, you saw my body as it was formed. I praise you because you made me in an amazing and wonderful way."

Even in the hidden space of a mother's body, God sees and knows your child. God already knows who your child will become. He loves your child more than you do, even if you don't think that's possible.

It's possible that like me, you struggled to conceive for quite a while. It's hard to imagine why God would keep women from conceiving, but often in the Bible, this withholding was all part of His glorious plan. Thank God today for blessing you with a child, caring for it, and loving it before you even knew you were pregnant.

L I S T E N

"Masterpiece" by Sandi Patty

Bed Rest Survival Tip

Hang your ultrasound photos in your room and praise God for such an amazing creation, which you are able to see in the secret place. Also, pray for mothers who have unwanted pregnancies. Not all women are ready for the gift of life God has given to them. Pray that they will grow to love the child as much as God does.

3

A Mother to Your
Unborn Baby

For you created my inmost being; you knit me together in
my mother's womb. I praise you because I am fearfully and
wonderfully made; your works are wonderful, I know that full
well. My frame was not hidden from you when I was made
in the secret place. When I was woven together in the depths of
the earth, your eyes saw my unformed body. All the days for
me were written in your book before one of them came to be.

—PSALM 139:13–16

Before I formed you in the womb, I knew you.
Before you were born I set you apart.

—JEREMIAH 1:5

You did not choose me, but I chose you and appointed you so
that you might go and bear fruit— fruit that will last.

—JOHN 15:16

For we are God's handiwork, created in Christ Jesus to do
good works, which God prepared in advance for us to do.

—EPHESIANS 2:10

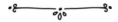

STACEY PYLMAN

Is this your first baby growing inside you? Have you been pregnant before? As soon as God puts a life inside you, you are a mother. You are caring for this life before you even know you are pregnant. Once you know you are pregnant, you start caring for your child by taking vitamins, getting good sleep, and eating healthier. Later in the pregnancy, many women start nesting by preparing their homes for the child to come. As a mom on bed rest, you are already sacrificing for this baby—giving up your freedom and mobility to do what's best for him or her. Yes, you are already a mother to this unborn baby, and your love is strong. Do you already feel that motherly protection?

This relationship reminds me of God's love for us. He loved us before we were born, before we were even created! Your heart and the heartbeat of your baby inside beat for God. He created us for His purpose, and He chose us before we chose Him. What comfort we can take in that truth! He loved us before we came into this world, knowing all the wrong we would do, knowing how sinful we would be, yet He still loved us enough to give us life and save us. Amazing love!

L I S T E N

"Deep in Love with You" by Michael W. Smith
"Oh How I Love You" by Zacardi Cortez

Bed Rest Survival Tip

Take some time to write a love letter to your baby or babies. Tell them how much you already love them and what you are doing for them because of that love. Tell them your hopes and dreams for them. Tell them how much God loves them, even more than you do!

4

The Days Are Long, but the Years Fly By

> But I trust in you, Lord; I say, "You are my
> God." My times are in your hands.
>
> —PSALM 31:14-15

> The end of a matter is better than its beginning, and patience
> is better than pride ... Do not say, "Why were the old days
> better than these?" For it is not wise to ask such questions.
>
> —ECCLESIASTES 7:8, 10

> But do not forget this one thing, dear friends:
> With the Lord a day is like a thousand years,
> and a thousand years are like a day.
>
> —2 PETER 3:8

Time moves so slowly when you are on bed rest. The days are so long! When you don't have anything to do or anywhere to be and you are just still, the days all bleed into one, and you realize you hardly know what day of the week it is unless you look at a calendar. In this day and age, we are used to very busy lives.

Slowing down or just sitting isn't something we are used to, and it can seem like your days on bed rest take forever.

I felt the same way when I was staying home with my triplets. The days were so long as I spent day after day bottle-feeding and changing diapers. The monotony, combined with my inability to leave the house much, made the days seem so long. But after my girls were a few years old, I looked back and thought, *Wow, that time home with those babies just flew by!*

When I was on bed rest, I started a blog and continued it through the first five years of my girls' lives. I appropriately gave it the title *The Bed Rest Blog: The Days Are Long, but the Years Fly By*. Your time on bed rest will seem short when you look back at it. Your time with the little babies and toddlers will seem to have gone by so fast when you reminisce.

It's funny how we experience time as humans. It's very different from how God experiences time. He is not bound by time. The Bible says that for God "a day is a thousand years and a thousand years are like a day" (2 Peter 3:8). We feel that same way about those early years with our kids. I suspect that someday when we meet our Maker, we will look back on our entire lives and think about how fast those years went by. Our time on earth is short, and we need to make the best of it for the glory of God.

L I S T E N

"Remember Me" by Mark Schultz
"Keep Me in the Moment" by Jeremy Camp

Bed Rest Survival Tip

———— ℰ • ℰ ————

Start a social media page or blog to share with others what is going on with you while you're on bed rest. You can share your daily challenges and your faith. You can be witty, uplifting, or authentic with your struggles. Use your story for God's kingdom. However, also be careful about how much you share publicly in this sinful world.

5

Why Is It Called "Morning Sickness"?

The Lord sustains them on their sickbed and restores them from their bed of illness.

—PSALM 41:3

Heal me, Lord, and I will be healed; save me and I will be saved, for you are the one I praise.

—JEREMIAH 17:14

Dear friend, I pray that you may enjoy good health and that all may go well with you, even as your soul is getting along well.

—3 JOHN 1:2

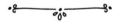

I had such bad morning sickness when I was pregnant with my triplets. I remember thinking, *Why do they call it "morning sickness"? It is all-day sickness!* The only thing I could eat was peanut butter and jelly toast, so it became my breakfast, lunch, and dinner. After weeks of sickness and one visit to the hospital for fluids and anti-nausea meds, I was so excited when the nausea left around fifteen weeks into my pregnancy. I didn't think I could have handled the sickness much longer.

Isn't it humbling that in our illness we realize how helpless we are and how dependent we really are on God? I remember praying heavily next to my toilet for God to just take the sickness away ... or give me the strength to get through it.

Now you are in a bed, possibly sick again (if you are on magnesium sulfate) and pleading with God again. *Please take it away ... or give me the strength to make it through.* God doesn't delight in our illness. He knows our pain when we are sick. Because of the sin in this world, we are plagued with sickness, but this wasn't God's plan for creation. God does promise, however, to be our comfort and strength during these times. When I was sitting by the toilet, I imagined Jesus was there by my side, rubbing my back, holding my hair, and telling me, "It's going to be okay; I'll help you get through this."

If you are blessed to be without sickness during your pregnancy, thank God for giving you health and strength. If you are battling illness, thank God for sustaining you, comforting you, and giving an end to this battle. God will restore you.

L I S T E N

"Before the Morning" by Josh Wilson
"God of My Everything" by Bebo Norman

Bed Rest Survival Tip

———— 8·8 ————

Don't be afraid to ask people *not* to visit if you are having a bad day (tired, sad, sick, and so forth). Also, don't be afraid to ask them to leave. Sometimes I told a lingering visitor that I was going to use the bathroom and that it took a while, so it would be great if he or she came back to visit at a different time. Visitors are only there to encourage you, and they don't want to be a burden. They will understand.

6

Just Keep Praying

Ask and it will be given to you; seek and you will
find; knock and the door will be opened to you.
—MATTHEW 7:7

Devote yourselves to prayer, being watchful and thankful.
—COLOSSIANS 4:2

You desire but do not have … You do not
have, because you do not ask God.
—JAMES 4:2

Confess your sins to each other and pray for each
other so that you may be healed. The prayer of a
righteous man is powerful and effective.
—JAMES 5:16

This is the confidence we have in approaching God: that
if we ask anything according to his will, he hears us.
And if we know that he hears us—whatever we ask—
we know that we have what we asked of him.
—1 JOHN 5:14–15

As Christians we often forget the power of prayer. I find it easy to ask for what I want in prayer. "God, please keep these babies safe. Help me feel better." Yes, God calls us to petition Him in prayer for all our desires and needs. But prayer is so much more than just asking God for what we want. God wants to have a conversation with us. He wants us to talk with Him like we would a highly respected friend. He wants us to share our trials, worries, and needs—but He also wants us to thank Him for the blessings He has given us and to be in awe of His work in our lives. You see, God already knows what we want and need. He wants us to pray so we connect with Him, so we see what He has done for us and recognize He is our provider—our source for everything.

The power of prayer is real, and God wants us to pray. He wants us to ask Him to supply our needs, but when we ask, we need to recognize that God knows what is best for us. He wants us to pray not for His benefit but for ours. The power of prayer isn't just getting what we ask for. The power of prayer is the fact that when we pray, we focus on God. We focus on what matters in life. We focus on our blessings. We focus on others' needs and gain perspective. All these things help our souls. Yes, pray for your own needs. Pray for your child or children, but don't neglect all the other powerful parts of prayer. Begin praying and watch how God feeds your soul.

L I S T E N

"Power of Prayer" by Matthew West
"God Who Listens" by Chris Tomlin

Bed Rest Survival Tip

———— •• ————

Start a prayer journal in a small notebook. First, write down what you are thankful for. I have found over the years that focusing on gratitude daily really lifts your spirit. Next, write any confessions you have, asking for forgiveness for any sins you have committed (even being short with your nurse or mother-in-law). Then write about your worries. Lastly, write down prayer requests you have for others and yourself.

7

Why Me?

I will instruct you and teach you in the way you should
go; I will counsel you with my loving eye on you.
—PSALM 32:8

Trust in the Lord with all your heart and lean not on
your own understanding; in all your ways submit
to him, and he will make your paths straight.
—PROVERBS 3:5–6

"For I know the plans I have for you," declares the Lord, "plans to
prosper you and not to harm you, plans to give you hope and a future."
—JEREMIAH 29:11

And we know that in all things God works for the good of those
who love him, who have been called according to his purpose.
—ROMANS 8:28

In this you greatly rejoice, though now for a little while you may
have had to suffer grief in all kinds of trials. These have come so that
the proven genuineness of your faith— of greater worth than gold …
may result in praise, glory and honor when Jesus Christ is revealed.
—1 PETER 1:6–7

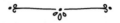

I remember when I was told I was having triplets. I was shocked and thought, *How could this be happening to me?* My question "Why me?" was one of excitement. But when I was told I was going to have to sit on bed rest for a long time, I also asked, "Why me?" This time I wasn't asking out of excitement because I had been chosen, but I was asking why I had to do this—why I had to sit for days and days when I knew of other moms of multiples who had never gone on bed rest.

God can choose to bless us with things we don't deserve, and our response might be "Why me? Who am I?" And God can choose to let challenges and tough times come into our lives, and we might cry out, "Why me?" As Christians we never really need to ask, "Why me?" We already know the answer. God chose us. It's part of His plan for us. God chose us to live lives with and for Him. God chooses to bless us. He chooses to challenge us. He chooses us to grow us from the challenges. God also chooses to help us through the challenges. We simply need to stop questioning and respond, "OK, Lord, I am Yours. I will do what You ask."

When we say we will follow Jesus, sometimes we don't know what that entails. It means we will trust that God has the best plan for our lives, that we will listen to God and follow His plan—even when it gets hard. Today recommit your life to follow God's will. Trust that He has a perfect plan for you and that you don't have to ask, "Why me?" because He knows.

L I S T E N

"Your Plans for Us" by Eleventh Hour Worship
"Who Am I" by Point of Grace

Bed Rest Survival Tip

———— 𝔤•𝔤 ————

You aren't the only one God has chosen for bed rest. Find solace from others who have been there. Find bed rest support groups and online forums (e.g., Sidelines.org and Keepemcookin.com). There are also good books out there from women who have been there (e.g., *Twelve Times Two: The Journey of a Mother on Bed Rest* by Jamie Giordano).

8

How Do I Choose a Name?

He determines the number of the stars
and calls them each by name.
—PSALM 147:4

A good name is more desirable than great riches;
to be esteemed is better than silver or gold.
—PROVERBS 22:1

Do not fear, for I have redeemed you; I have
summoned you by name, you are mine.
—ISAIAH 43:1

How many baby name books have you pored through? Isn't it difficult trying to choose a name your child will have for the rest of his or her life? Some names seem too childish, some seem too old, and others remind you of someone you don't like. Suddenly it hits you … Yes! That is the perfect name!

God has always placed importance on a person's name. There are a couple of reasons names have so much importance.

First, God, the Creator of this immense universe, knows *our* names. He uses our names to call us. "Fear not, for I have redeemed you; I have summoned you by name, you are mine." We have become children of God. He knows our names, and we know His voice.

A name is also valuable in the context of reputation. "A good name is more desirable than great riches; to be esteemed is better than silver or gold" (Proverbs 22:1). However, God isn't concerned about our worldly reputations. Our value in His eyes isn't measured by our popularity, money, possessions, career esteem, or status. Our names are measured as good by our lives in Christ. Our service to both God and others as well as our compassion, strength of character, and godly wisdom are the benchmarks of a good name in Christ.

What will people think when they hear your name? What reputation does your name have in Christ's kingdom? What reputation will your child's name have in Christ's kingdom? Say a prayer now for your child, that he or she will serve the Lord with a good name.

L I S T E N

"He Knows My Name" by Paul Baloche
"You Know My Name" by Tasha Cobbs
Leonard (featuring Jimi Cravity)
"He Knows My Name" by Francesca Battistelli

Bed Rest Survival Tip

———— ❧•❧ ————

Spend your time on bed rest with those baby name books. You have time to go through all the names and find the perfect one for your child. It's also fun to investigate the meanings behind names.

9

The Healing
Power of Music

My lips will shout for joy when I sing praise
to you— I, whom you have delivered.

—PSALM 71:23

I will praise the Lord all my life; I will sing
praise to my God as long as I live.

—PSALM 146:2

Be filled with the spirit, speaking to one another with psalms,
hymns and songs from the spirit. Sing and make music
from your heart to the Lord, always giving thanks to God the
Father for everything, in the name of our Lord Jesus Christ.

—EPHESIANS 5:18-20

Is any one of you in trouble? Let them pray. Is
anyone happy? Let them sing songs of praise.

—JAMES 5:13

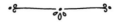

One of my favorite things to do on bed rest was listening to
music. iPods were newly invented, and my friend brought me

hers with a speaker so I could listen. There was just something nice about turning off the television and simply listening to music for a while.

I love music, and it's amazing to me how much music is part of our lives. I can hear a song on the radio, and it brings me right back to a time and place. Maybe it's a song that reminds me of a vacation, a song I sang at a baptism, or a sad song I listened to over and over again when I broke up with a guy. Music brings out our emotions—feelings of sadness, joy, peace, and excitement. Music can also be very healing. Listening to calming music can bring down stress and anxiety. Listening to sad music can bring out tears and a needed cry. Songs can inspire us to work hard, keep going, or keep trying.

Music is so beautiful; there is no surprise that God created it. When music is referenced in the Bible, people were using it to praise God. It's a way to connect not only with our emotions but also with God. It is a way to worship and experience His beautiful gift to us. Right now, as you sit on bed rest, you will have days when you feel very different emotions. Listening to music can help you connect with those emotions or even change your emotions for the better. The type of music you listen to does matter, so choose wisely for yourself and the Lord. Use music to worship God daily. Turn it up and sing along.

Bed Rest Survival Tip

——— ✼•✼ ———

- Turn off the TV a couple of times a day and just listen to music.
- Try out different genres and see whether there is something you like and didn't know.

- If you are tired of talking and words, listen to soothing instrumental music, close your eyes, and daydream.
- It's best to listen to uplifting music if possible. I find praise and worship music to be the most uplifting, but you can also sing many secular love songs in worship to God or pretend He is singing them to you! ☺

STACEY'S UPLIFTING PLAYLIST

"Happy" by Pharrell Williams
"Somewhere over the Rainbow" by Israel "IZ" Kamakawiwo'ole
"We Are Brave" by Shawn McDonald
"Stronger" by Kelly Clarkson
"I'm a Believer" by The Monkees
"I Will Survive" by Gloria Gaynor
"Stronger" by Mandisa
"Geronimo" by Sheppard
"Walking on Sunshine" by Katrina & The Waves
"Up Again" by Dan Bremnes
"(Your Love Keeps Lifting Me) Higher and Higher" by Jackie Wilson
"Ain't No Mountain High Enough" by Marvin Gaye & Tammi Terrell
"You Lead" by Jamie Grace
"Don't Worry Be Happy" by Bobby McFerrin
"Three Little Birds" by Bob Marley & The Wailers or Elizabeth Mitchell
"Don't Give Up on Me" by Andy Grammar
"The One Thing" by Paul Colman
"In the Mood" by Glenn Miller and His Orchestra

"Thrive" by Casting Crowns
"I'm Gonna Be (500 Miles)" by The Proclaimers
"Good Feeling" by Austin French
"These Are Days" by 10,000 Maniacs
"Days Like This" by Van Morrison
"Have a Little Faith in Me" by John Hiatt
"Can't Stop the Feeling!" by Justin Timberlake
"See the Light" by TobyMac
"What a Wonderful World" by Louis Armstrong
"Old Church Choir" by Zach Williams
"Lovely Day" by Bill Withers
"Reason" by Unspoken
"I'm Alright" by Jo Dee Messina
"Let It Be" by The Beatles
"Sing a Song" by Earth, Wind & Fire
"Livin' on a Prayer" by Bon Jovi
"I Found You" by Andy Grammar
"Shoulders" by for KING & COUNTRY
"Open Your Eyes" by Daybreaker (featuring Elliot LaRue & Tyler
   Sjostrom)
"Center of It" by Chris August
"Champion" by Carrie Underwood
"Rise Up" by Andra Day
"I Will Wait" by Mumford & Sons
"Today Is Beautiful" by David Dunn
"Keep Your Head Up" by Andy Grammar
"O-o-h Child" by The Five Stairsteps
"(Sittin' on) the Dock of the Bay" by Ottis Redding
"I Wanna Dance with Somebody" by Whitney Houston
"Fight Song" by Rachel Platten
"He Still Does (Miracles)" by Hawk Nelson
"Home" by Phillip Phillips
"Roar" by Katy Perry
"Sparrow" by Audrey Assad

"Mama Said" by Mica Paris
"Hold My Hand" by Jess Glynne
"You Can't Hurry Love" by The Supremes
"Send Me on My Way" by Rusted Root
"Hold on Tight" by Aloe Blacc
"When the Saints" by Sara Groves
"One Moment in Time" by Whitney Houston
"Haven't Met You Yet" by Michael Bublé
"Stand by Me" by Ben E. King
"I Can See Clearly Now" by Johnny Nash
"Your Wings" by Lauren Daigle
"Don't Stop Believin'" by Journey
"You Gotta Be" by Des'ree
"I Will Be" by Wynonna
"No Impossible with You" by I Am They
"Good Vibrations" by The Beach Boys
"Here Comes the Sun" by The Beatles
"Hero" by Mariah Carey
"Good Morning" by Mandisa (featuring TobyMac)
"God Gave Me You" by Dave Barnes
"Take My Hand" by Shawn McDonald
"Survivor" by Destiny's Child
"I'm a Survivor" by Reba McEntire
"Smile" by Sidewalk Prophets
"You Raise Me Up" by Josh Groban
"Bridge Over Troubled Water" by Simon & Garfunkel
"Sky Spills Over" by Michael W. Smith
"When You Believe" by Whitney Houston and Mariah Carey
"Lean on Me" by Sandro Cavazza
"Better Days" by Ant Clemons and Justin Timberlake
"Reach" by Peter Furler
"Put Your Records On" by Corinne Bailey Rae
"Yes He Can" by CAIN
"Never Gonna Let You Down" by Colbie Caillat

"Close to You" by R3HAB & Andy Grammar
"Color Me in Sunshine" by P!nk & Willow Sage Heart
"River of Life" by Mac Powell
"Go Down Singing" by Tim Be Told

10
God Loves Life

God blessed them and said to them, "Be
fruitful and increase in number."
—GENESIS 1:28

With blessings of the skies above, blessings of the deep
springs below, blessings of the breast and womb.
—GENESIS 49:25

Children are a heritage from the Lord, offspring a reward from
him. Like arrows in the hands of a warrior are children born in
one's youth. Blessed is the man whose quiver is full of them.
—PSALM 127:3-5

Your wife will be like a fruitful vine within your house;
your children will be like olive shoots around your table. Yes,
this will be the blessing for the man who fears the Lord.
—PSALM 128:3-4

My husband wanted two kids, so the news of triplets was a little
shocking to him. The national average of children per family in
the United States is 2.5. With the increasing costs of caring for

children and the many ways to prevent conception, families are much smaller than they were just decades ago. People often look at families with four or more children and think they are crazy. But the truth is ... God loves life!

God commanded us in Genesis to be fruitful and increase in number. He values life and more Christians here on this earth to glorify and live as a testament to Him. He is the Author and Creator of life, and humans were created as something very good. Some people ask why God would want more sinful people on this earth. Or why would He want us to bring children into a sinful world? He doesn't want more sin. He wants to bring love and goodness to the world. He wants more Christians to be witnesses to unbelievers. He is expanding His kingdom.

Children are a reward from Him, the giver of life. Many women, including myself, struggled to conceive a baby and probably wondered why a God who loves life so much would make it so hard. Were we underserving of a reward? However, because He is the Author and Creator of life, only He decides when to give life and when to take it away. His ways are often beyond our understanding, and we need to trust His good and perfect ways. Thank God today for His gift of life in your womb.

L I S T E N

"For This Child" by Ken Blount
"The Blessing" by Kari Jobe and Cody Carnes

Bed Rest Survival Tip

———— ❧·❧ ————

Today pray for the many mothers and fathers who struggle to conceive children. If you know of any personally, write them a note of encouragement.

11
How Big Is This Baby Going to Get?

But blessed is the one who trusts in the Lord, whose confidence
is in him. They will be like a tree planted by the water that
sends out its roots by the stream. It does not fear when
heat comes; its leaves are always green. It has no worries
in a year of drought and never fails to bear fruit.

—JEREMIAH 17:7-8

"I am the vine; you are the branches. If you
remain in me and I in you, you will bear much
fruit; apart from me you can do nothing."

—JOHN 15:5

So then, just as you received Christ Jesus as Lord, continue to live
your lives in him, rooted and built up in him, strengthened in the
faith as you were taught, and overflowing with thankfulness.

—COLOSSIANS 2:6-7

Like newborn babies, crave pure spiritual milk, so
that by it you may grow up in your salvation, now
that you have tasted that the Lord is good.

—1 PETER 2:2

Grow in the grace and knowledge of our Lord and Savior Jesus Christ. To him be the glory both now and forever! Amen.

—2 PETER 3:18

God is a God of growth. He created plants, animals, and people to grow physically. Every living thing in creation grows. Creation isn't designed to be stagnant. For God's creation to grow, it needs nourishment (food and water), time, and space. Right now, you are giving nourishment, time, and space for your baby to grow. What a beautiful thing that God designed us to be able to do this for our babies. You are on bed rest right now because you are trying to give your baby more time to grow. What a loving sacrifice!

Now, let's apply that to spiritual growth. God also wants us to grow spiritually. In the Bible, He tells us to be like a tree planted by water with roots reaching into nourishment. That means God wants us to read our Bibles, do devotions, pray, and worship with other believers as nourishment for our spiritual growth. We should crave this kind of spiritual "milk" so we can grow in the grace and knowledge of our Savior and bear fruit in His kingdom. God wants us to stay attached to Him so we can grow spiritually, like an unborn baby attached by an umbilical cord receives nourishment from his or her mother.

Someday you are going to want your baby to stop growing so fast. It's funny how we want to keep things the same and keep our kids little. But the truth is that God created our kids to grow and mature in their faith. Today you are watching as the baby develops eyelids, eyebrows, and senses. In the future, you watch as your child develops faith and a heart for the hurting. It's all part of God's growth plan.

L I S T E N

"Slow Down" by Nichole Nordeman
"The Benediction" by Timothy James Meaney

Bed Rest Survival Tip

Keep track of your baby's growth. Hang up ultrasound photos of your baby. Keep measuring your belly. Want to know how big your baby is getting and what he or she developed this week? There are many apps out there to track your pregnancy, such as the following:

- Pregnancy Tracker: Baby Bump
- Pregnancy App by Amila
- Pregnancy+
- The Bump Pregnancy
- Sprout Pregnancy
- What to Expect Pregnancy & Baby Tracker App

12
God's Work within You

*I prayed for this child, and the Lord has granted me
what I asked of him. So now I give him to the Lord. For
his whole life he will be given over to the Lord.*
—1 SAMUEL 1:27-28

*"For I know the plans I have for you," declares
the Lord, "plans to prosper you and not to harm
you, plans to give you hope and a future."*
—JEREMIAH 29:11

Every good and perfect gift is from above.
—JAMES 1:17

Do you often wonder about the miracle growing inside you? Who
is this person you will meet soon? What will he or she be like?
What will he or she be when all grown up? What will be his or her
favorites? Will she be like me? Will he be like his dad? God already
knows the answers to those questions and many more. God has
created your child for a very specific purpose in His kingdom. He
also created your child in His image so she or he might be like his
or her Creator.

What does it mean that your child has a God-given purpose in this world? It means God has already created your child in His image with gifts and talents that will help him or her accomplish his or her God-given life plans. God knows your child better than you ever will, and He loves him or her even more than you can imagine. Whether your child's life is short or long, he or she has a purpose in God's kingdom.

God created you in the same way. Before you were even born, God had a plan and purpose for you. Are you living out God's plans for your life? How do you know? Do you ask Him daily what it is He wants you to do? Take time now to pray and ask God what His will is for your life. Ask Him to reveal it and guide your steps. Surrender your life and the life of your child to Him—His will and purpose.

L I S T E N

"Image of God" by We Are Messengers
"I Surrender All" by Carrie Underwood

Bed Rest Survival Tip

Ask friends and family to guess your baby's birthdate, pounds and ounces, length, and hair color (if any). It will be fun to see who was closest.

13

This Is a Marathon, Not a Sprint

He gives strength to the weary and increases the power of
the weak ... But those who hope in the Lord will renew their
strength. They will soar on wings like eagles; they will run
and not grow weary, they will walk and not be faint.

—ISAIAH 40:29, 31

Do you not know that in a race all the runners run, but only
one gets the prize? Run in such a way as to get the prize.

—1 CORINTHIANS 9:24

Therefore, since we are surround by such a great cloud
of witnesses, let us throw off everything that hinders
and the sin that so easily entangles. And let us run
with perseverance the race marked out for us.

—HEBREWS 12:1

May the God of peace ... equip you with everything good for
doing his will, and may he work in us what is pleasing to him,
through Jesus Christ, to whom be glory for ever and ever. Amen.

—HEBREWS 13:20-21

STACEY PYLMAN

Did you know you are running a race right now? It doesn't seem like you are running a race when your only exercise is walking to the bathroom; however, it is a race nonetheless. This race is a mental marathon. It is a long, sometimes grueling race, but just like a marathon, the prize at the finish line is so worth the runner's numb feet, side aches, illness, as well as mental and physical exhaustion.

There are many friends and family on the sidelines cheering you on as you run this marathon. They are holding up signs, encouraging you. But there is someone who is running the race with you, picking you up when you fall, and carrying you over the potholes. Not only did Jesus equip you for this race, but He is also running it with you. He is giving you the strength to do this. Do not rush the finish line; follow His pace.

Do not give up! Sometimes I would lie in bed and think, *Uncle! I can't do this anymore!* The truth is, I couldn't do it from the very beginning of the race, not without God's help. Even when I was running ahead of Jesus and thinking, *I am doing great with this pregnancy race. This is not so hard*, He was still there beside me, ready to help me when I tripped, fell, and held my hand out to ask for help. He is always there.

Pray to Jesus right now. Thank Him for running this race alongside you and ask Him to help you get to the finish line.

L I S T E N

"Run the Race" by Holly Starr
"Running" by Hillsong (Live)
"Run On" by Kara Coats (featuring Allie Ray)

Bed Rest Survival Tip

———— 8•8 ————

Athletes often post encouraging notes to themselves as they train for a big race. Take some time to write sticky notes that say phrases such as the following:

- "You can do this, Mom!"
- "Be strong!"
- "No pain, no gain!"
- "The finish line is just ahead!"

Search for more on the internet.

14

Unable to Care for My Family

These commandments that I give you today are to be upon your hearts. Impress them on your children. Talk about them when you sit at home and when you walk along the road, when you lie down and when you get up.

—DEUTERONOMY 6:6–7

Start children off on the way they should go, and even when they are old they will not turn from it.

—PROVERBS 22:6

She speaks with wisdom, and faithful instruction is on her tongue ... Her children arise and call her blessed; her husband also, and he praises her.

—PROVERBS 31:26, 28

As a mother comforts her child, so will I comfort you.

—ISAIAH 66:13

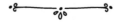

One of the most difficult issues for mothers on bed rest is that they cannot take care of their other child or children and have to rely on others to do this job for them. This change is extremely challenging for mothers. They are so used to taking care of everyone. And to make matters more difficult, often children don't understand why Mommy can't do things for them like she always did before. Some children seem to drift away from wanting their mom and ask for dad instead. This is all very normal for moms on bed rest.

Sometimes as moms we try to take control of everything, and we forget that really God is in control. Mothers have demanding jobs, but they are only human, and God knows that. You aren't superhuman, and you weren't created to be. You were created to have weaknesses, to need God, and to ask for His help. He knows you cannot do everything for your family right now, and your main job is to nurture the baby inside you.

The good news is that God has a perfect plan for your moment of need. He will take care of your loved ones. He will use your church community, friends, or family to step in when you cannot. Praise God for how He uses others in our lives to show love and care. So, take a deep breath and give some of your mothering tasks away. You can still keep the best ones like hugs, snuggles, kisses, stories, giggles, sharing Jesus, and prayers.

L I S T E N

"One Heartbeat at a Time" by Steven Curtis Chapman
"A Mother's Prayer" by Keith & Kristyn Getty

Bed Rest Survival Tip

——— 8·8 ———

Read books to your other younger children, such as the following:

- *Stuck in Bed: The Pregnancy Bed Rest Picture Book for Kids ... and Moms* by Jennifer Degl and Angela Davids
- *Bed Rest Mommy* by Jennifer Christiensen
- *Mommy Has to Stay in Bed* by Annette Rivlin-Gutman

Find activities you can do with your kids to spend quality time with them (the books above give some good ideas). Here are some examples:

- Make necklaces and add a bead for each day you are on bed rest.
- Write the number of days until you are due on sticky notes, toilet paper, or paper towels and let your child rip one off each day.
- Spread out an old sheet under you and your child and play with Play-Doh.
- Play board games.
- Ask someone to livestream or record your kids' events, which you are missing.
- Use Skype or FaceTime to do bedtime routine with your kids (stories and prayers).

15

The Kingdom of Heaven Belongs to Such as These

He called a little child to him, and placed the child among them.
And he said: "Truly I tell you, unless you change and become like
little children, you will never enter the kingdom of heaven ... And
whoever welcomes one such child in my name welcomes me."

—MATTHEW 18:2–5

Then people brought little children to Jesus for him to place his
hands on them and pray for them. But the disciples rebuked
them. Jesus said, "Let the little children come to me, and do not
hinder them, for the kingdom of heaven belongs to such as these."
When he had placed his hands on them, he went on from there.

—MATTHEW 19:13–15

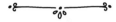

Babies are so precious ... and so helpless. They depend on someone
to give them nourishment, to care for every single one of their
needs. They don't try to do anything on their own. Their only
ability is to cry for help. Mothers soon realize *they* give their babies

what they need to survive. Early on, this becomes their priority and focus.

This is what Jesus meant when He told us to be like children to enter the kingdom of heaven. We need to admit we are helpless and totally dependent on God. Our only ability is to cry for help to the Lord. He is our source for survival. He meets all our needs. Until we recognize our helplessness and total dependence on Him, we cannot enter the kingdom of heaven.

Admitting our weakness and dependence is a very difficult thing to do in a world where we are praised for our accomplishments, independence, and strength. Jesus's message was one that turned the world upside down for the disciples and all His followers that day. Let it be a message that turns your world upside down today. Don't be ashamed of your dependence on the Lord. He alone can provide for *all* your needs and your baby's needs.

L I S T E N

"Jesus Loves Me" by Christy Nockels
"I Am Weak" by Craig Aven

Bed Rest Survival Tip

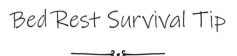

Don't be ashamed of all the ways you depend on God and others for your needs. Today write a list of all the things you can't do for yourself, things others do for you, and thank God for taking care of you.

16

Getting Bad News

For sighing has become my daily food; my groans
pour out like water. What I feared has come upon me;
what I dreaded has happened to me. I have no peace,
no quietness; I have no rest, but only turmoil.

—JOB 3:24–26

A righteous person may have many troubles,
but the Lord delivers him from them all.

—PSALM 34:19

They will have no fear of bad news; their hearts
are steadfast, trusting in the Lord.

—PSALM 112:7

You will keep in perfect peace those whose minds
are steadfast, because they trust in you.

—ISAIAH 26:3

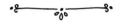

"There's a problem with the baby." These are words pregnant
moms fear. Words that can make the world stand still and your
heart burst in your chest. My sister experienced this. She was
sixteen weeks pregnant with her fourth child. She went to her

ultrasound, and there was no heartbeat. She was shocked and devastated; she couldn't process what they were saying to her. How could this be?

Many of you have heard or will hear some bad news while you are pregnant or even after you deliver. If you live long enough, you will hear bad news from doctors. What are we to do when bad news is delivered—when we are sent into a mix of shock and fear? The Bible tells us that when we get bad news, when our world implodes around us, we should trust Him. Trust Him—that's it. But it is extremely hard for us to do this. When we get bad news, our first instinct is *not* to trust. We flounder, flail, and give way to our fears, just like Peter walking to Jesus on the water. But even when we forget to trust, God will pick us up. He will remind us again to trust Him, and we will walk with Him again, realizing we will survive with God helping us, and we can trust that.

Later, when my sister had worked her way through grief and had found joy again, she explained to me that before losing her baby, she had always been living in fear. She knew she had a good life, and she saw others going through horrible circumstances. She told me she was always waiting for that "shoe to drop" and wondered whether she would be able to handle it. "Now I know I can handle it. God got me through. I've lost a lot of that fear now," she shared. She realized she could now trust God to carry her through the bad, and He will carry you too. If or when you get bad news, put your trust in God. Trust that He will carry you through it.

L I S T E N

"Find You Here" by Ellie Holcomb
"It Is Well with My Soul" by Audrey Assad or Anthem Lights

Bed Rest Survival Tip

Whenever I'm in fear, the words of old hymns I learned as a child pop into my head. They give me such peace because the words ring so true in my adult circumstances. Ask someone to bring you a hymnal. Often in the back, there is a list of songs organized by category. Look up hymns on trust, fear, help, and hope. Read the words of the hymns and be encouraged. If you don't have a hymnal, search the internet for hymns about trust and so forth.

17
What Good Does Worrying Do?

She is clothed with strength and dignity;
she can laugh at the days to come.
—PROVERBS 31:25

Can any one of you by worrying add a single hour to your life?
—MATTHEW 6:27

Then Jesus said to his disciples: "Therefore I tell you,
do not worry about your life, what you will eat; or
about your body, what you will wear. For life is more
than food, and the body more than clothes."
—LUKE 12:22–23

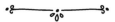

It's interesting how quickly your perspective changes when you are put in extreme circumstances. When I was first pregnant, I worried about having fashionable maternity clothes. I didn't want to look like a big tent, and sadly stylish clothes were important to me. When I was put on bed rest in the hospital, how quickly I gave up worrying about my clothes and reached for the pajamas and slippers. Clothes didn't matter anymore; life mattered, namely the lives growing inside me. My comfort and the comfort of the babies inside me became my first priority.

Generally, I have never been a big worrier. Sometimes I think it's because my mother worried enough for both of us. If worrying helped, she had it covered, and I wouldn't need to bother with it. While I watched others worry about my pregnancy, I just gave it to God and trusted ... and so did my mom.

So many times in life, we worry over such silly things. I often wonder how often God shakes His head with a smirk, like that all-knowing Father who knows His child is worrying for no reason. Sometimes we worry out of fear; sometimes it is because we are placing our focus on the wrong things in life. Either way, our worrying accomplishes nothing. Are we able to change anything by worrying?

God desires that we trust Him and in so doing give up our worries. Worrying right now can be detrimental to you and your baby, but trusting in the Lord will bring the calm, peace, and strength needed.

L I S T E N

"Sparrow" by Audrey Assad
"Sparrows" by Jason Gray

Bed Rest Survival Tip

———— 8•8 ————

Read and journal about the following quotes on worry:

Today is the tomorrow we worried about yesterday.
—AUTHOR UNKNOWN

Do not anticipate trouble or worry about what
may never happen. Keep in the sunlight.
—BENJAMIN FRANKLIN

If you want to test your memory, try to recall what
you were worrying about one year ago today.
—E. JOSEPH COSSMAN

Worrying is like a rocking chair, it gives you
something to do, but it gets you nowhere.
—GLENN TURNER

That the birds of worry and care fly over your
head, this you cannot change, but that they build
nests in your hair, this you can prevent.
—CHINESE PROVERB

A day of worry is more exhausting than a day of work.
—JOHN LUBBOCK

Heavy thoughts bring on physical maladies,
when the soul is oppressed so is the body.
—MARTIN LUTHER

I am an old man and have known a great many
troubles, but most of them never happened.
—MARK TWAIN

Blessed is the person who is too busy to worry in the
daytime and too sleepy to worry at night.
—AUTHOR UNKNOWN

Do not be afraid of tomorrow; for God is already there.
—AUTHOR UNKNOWN

Every evening I turn my worries over to God.
He's going to be up all night anyway.
—MARY C. CROWLEY

18

We Are Family

Yet to all who did receive him, to those who believed in
his name, he gave the right to become children of God—
children born not of natural descent, nor of human
decision or a husband's will, but born of God.

—JOHN 1:12–13

The Spirit himself testifies with our spirit, that we are God's
children. Now if we are children, then we are heirs—heirs
of God and co-heirs with Christ, if indeed we share in his
sufferings in order that we may also share in his glory.

—ROMANS 8:16–17

So in Christ Jesus you are all children of God through faith, for
all of you who were baptized into Christ have clothed yourselves
with Christ. There is neither Jew nor Gentile, neither slave nor free,
nor is there male and female, for you are all one in Christ Jesus.
If you belong to Christ, then you are Abraham's seed, and heirs
according to the promise ... So you are no longer a slave, but God's
child; and since you are his child, God has made you also an heir.

—GALATIANS 3:26–29; 4:7

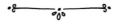

Until you have a child, you might not totally understand what it's like to love a family member unconditionally. If this is your first child, just wait and see. Family is an amazing concept God designed. He wants us to have responsible adults to raise and support us when we are most vulnerable. He uses family members to teach, guide, and raise us into adults who know Christ, follow Him, and work for His kingdom. Some are blessed to have great Christian family members to raise them, but not everyone does. This world is broken and sinful, so that means families will be too. Family members aren't perfect, and they often challenge us in ways no one else can. But God often has plans for others to step in as substitute family members in the lives of those without a great family example and to act as a loving family would.

All of us have a different family tree, and the branches of our tree are all parts of God's design for our family. Whether there are broken branches, branches grafted in, or unknown branches, God uses them for our good and growth. He planned where you were going to come from, and He will use you for His purposes no matter what family you came from or what family adopts you.

In the end, when we are together in heaven someday, it won't matter who our biological family members are. God said we all belong to Christ and have been adopted as His sons or daughters. We have the greatest family member, Jesus, who is there to raise us at our most vulnerable—while living here on earth. He will teach, guide, raise us, and love us unconditionally the same way we love our children.

L I S T E N

"Children of God" by Third Day
"Family of God" by Newsboys

Bed Rest Survival Tip

———— 8•8 ————

Work on filling in a baby book for your unborn child. Fill in that family tree. You could even draw or paint a tree on paper and then have family members put fingerprints on the branches in various colored stamp ink to make them look like fall leaves. You could label the fingerprints with the names of the family members. Frame the artwork and hang it in the nursery.

19

It Should Be Called "Bed Restless"!

The Lord replied, "My Presence will go with
you, and I will give you rest."

—EXODUS 33:14

In peace I will lie down and sleep, for you
alone, Lord, make me dwell in safety.

—PSALM 4:8

Return to your rest, my soul, for the Lord has been good to you.

—PSALM 116:7

Come to me, all you who are weary and burdened, and I will give
you rest. Take my yoke upon you and learn from me, for I am
gentle and humble in heart, and you will find rest for your souls.

—MATTHEW 11:28-29

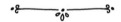

Having to use the bathroom every few hours, getting vitals checked
all through the night, being unable to roll over to get comfortable,
having a sore butt and hips—you name it. They should call this
"bed restless"! I remember wishing I could get good sleep during the

night while on bed rest, but every pregnant woman knows it's nearly impossible to get good sleep while pregnant, let alone in a hospital. God created us to need rest. He created the Sabbath day to give us rest from our work. Rest was part of God's plan from the beginning. Our bodies need sleep to regain strength, and pregnant bodies require even more. Remember that first trimester when you were tired all the time? Sleeping rest gives us a break from talking, thinking, and hopefully worrying—if we give it over to God.

I love that God promises rest to the weary and burdened. He gives rest to our bodies and souls. Not only does He give us rest; He protects us as we rest. While we sleep, God never sleeps. He keeps watch over us, and we never leave His hands. What a great way to fall asleep every night, knowing that while you sleep, God is holding you in His hands. "I lie down and sleep; I wake again, because the Lord sustains me" (Psalm 3:5).

L I S T E N

"Restless" by Audrey Assad
"I Will Rest in You" by Jaci Velasquez

Bed Rest Survival Tip

If you don't have enough pillows, ask for more. If you are in a hospital, ask your nurses or visitors for them. If you are at home, ask your spouse to search for the perfect pillow combination for your comfort. Sometimes finding the perfect pillow positions can be difficult to master, but you have the time.

20

Bed Worship

How great you are, Sovereign Lord! There is no one like you, and there is no God but you, as we have heard with our own ears.

—2 SAMUEL 7:22

Therefore my heart is glad and my tongue rejoices; my body also will rest secure.

—PSALM 16:9

Because your love is better than life, my lips will glorify you. I will praise you as long as I live, and in your name I will lift up my hands.

—PSALM 63:3-4

It is good to praise the Lord and make music to your name, O Most High, proclaiming your love in the morning and your faithfulness at night

—PSALM 92:1-2

Come, let us bow down in worship, let us kneel before the Lord our Maker.

—PSALM 95:6

Lord, you are my God; I will exalt you and praise your name, for in perfect faithfulness you have done marvelous things, things planned long ago.

—ISAIAH 25:1

How do you usually worship? Do you go to a church? Do you sing praises or meditate on the Bible? Do you take time to list the things you are thankful for in prayer? Sometimes when you sit in bed day after day, your old routines are lost. You can forget to do things like brush your teeth, cut your toenails, and even spend time worshipping the Lord. Sometimes we don't feel like worshipping because nothing seems right or happy.

It seems odd to worship in bed, and it may even seem difficult when you are facing some scary circumstances. However, worship brings us close to the One who takes care of all our circumstances. Praise God with broken hallelujahs. Don't neglect time spent worshipping the Lord, for "when your tongue rejoices your body will rest secure" (Psalm 16:9).

Take some time to worship today. Listen to praise songs or spend time in thankful prayer. Reflect on times God has been there for you in the past and carried you through. You will be surprised by how God will lift your spirit through communion with Him.

LISTEN

"Broken Hallelujah" by Mandisa
"Behold Our God" by Sovereign Grace Music
"Be Unto Your Name/Holy, Holy, Holy" by Brian Doerksen

Bed Rest Survival Tip

———— 8•8 ————

Being on bed rest, you have a strange advantage to see the many blessings you have in your life. Being deprived of the freedoms you once enjoyed has opened your eyes to the many blessings you once took for granted. Use this time to thank God for all the things you appreciate anew. Begin a list of all you are thankful for. Add to this list daily. It can serve as a way of worshipping, and it will help you remember to be grateful once you are off bed rest someday.

21
God's Helping Hands

The Lord is my strength and my shield; my
heart trusts in him, and he helps me.

—PSALM 28:7

God is our refuge and strength, an ever-present help in trouble.

—PSALM 46:1

Yet I am always with you; you hold me by my right hand.

—PSALM 73:23

So do not fear, for I am with you; do not be dismayed,
for I am your God. I will strengthen you and help you;
I will uphold you with my righteous right hand.

—ISAIAH 41:10

Think back to when you were a child, holding your mom or dad's hand as you walked through a busy mall or as you jumped into the water. Do you remember the safety and security a hand gave you? For some reason, holding their hand meant you were safe because they would take care of anything that came your way. Their hand would guide you safely through crowds and keep you from drowning. Maybe someone held your hand as you had to do something you were scared about. There was no real power coming through that hand, but the contact provided security—knowing someone was there with you.

Now think about who has been holding your hand over these past few months as you have walked around pregnant. Most likely it was someone who cares for you: a spouse, a friend, a family member, or a nurse. They held your hand to help you, show you love, and provide you safety. But they aren't the only ones holding your hand.

God tells us in the Bible that He holds us in His hands. He is our help, safety, and love. Right now you and your baby are being held in His hands, and you will never slip through. You are never safer than when you are in God's grip, and no one can provide more help than His hands. God's hands have power. Rest easy in them.

L I S T E N

"Lift Me Up" by The Afters
"Reach" by Peter Furler
"Take My Hand" by Shawn McDonald

Bed Rest Survival Tip

While you are listening to these songs, think about God's hands reaching out and holding you. Trace your hands on paper and hang it by your bed to remind yourself that God is holding you.

22
Drink, Drink, Drink!

My soul thirsts for God, for the living God.
When can I go and meet with God?
—PSALM 42:2

Come, all you who are thirsty, come to the waters.
—ISAIAH 55:1

Jesus answered, "Everyone who drinks this water will be
thirsty again, but whoever drinks the water I give them
will never thirst. Indeed, the water I give them will become
in them a spring of water welling up to eternal life."
—JOHN 4:13-14

On the last and greatest day of the festival, Jesus stood
and said in a loud voice, "Let anyone who is thirsty come
to me and drink. Whoever believes in me, as Scripture has
said, rivers of living water will flow from within them."
—JOHN 7:37-38

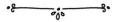

Doctors tell us it is super important for pregnant women to stay hydrated, so we drink. Do you feel like you are drowning in all the water you have to drink? It's so hard to drink all the water you are supposed to when your stomach is being squished by the baby (or in my case, babies). It's amazing to me how good water is for us. I'm quick to get dehydrated, and I know drinking water is good for me, but I still struggle with doing it enough.

It's no surprise that Jesus chose water as a symbol for His Spirit. Water is vital to our bodies. It is something we can't live without. When Jesus talked about water that would satisfy all our needs and flow from us, He meant the Holy Spirit. We need the Holy Spirit more than we need water! We cannot live without God within us. Yes, we could physically live, but we wouldn't really be living. Only Jesus can give us living water—eternal life. Graciously receive living water from Jesus today and ask the Holy Spirit to fill you.

L I S T E N

"Living Waters" by Keith & Kristyn Getty
"God So Loved" by We The Kingdom
"Thrive" by Casting Crowns

Bed Rest Survival Tip

Keep water by you at all times. Maybe even use an app to remind you to drink. Motivational water bottles with time markers can also help. Hydration keeps contractions away. It's one of the best things you can do besides resting. Plus, the more you drink, the more you need to pee … and then you can get out of bed and stretch! ;)

23

Nurses Are a Gift from God

For I was hungry and you gave me something to eat, I was thirsty and you gave me something to drink, I was a stranger and you invited me in, I needed clothes and you clothed me, I was sick and you looked after me, I was in prison and you came to visit me.

—MATTHEW 25:35–36

But a Samaritan, as he traveled, came where the man was; and when he saw him, he took pity on him. He went to him and bandaged his wounds, pouring on oil and wine. Then he put the man on his own donkey, brought him to an inn and took care of him.

—LUKE 10:33–34

And my God will meet all your needs according to the riches of his glory in Christ Jesus.

—PHILIPPIANS 4:19

I loved my nurses! I mean it. They listened to my fears, helped me shower, changed my sheets, massaged my back, laughed with me, encouraged me, and watched over my babies and me closely. I still remember my nurses' names fifteen years later. When people say nurses are angels in disguise, they aren't kidding.

I think the reason we love nurses so much is because they demonstrate what it means to be the hands and feet of Jesus. They are the embodiment of care. My nurses cared for me in ways I never would have expected, and I was truly grateful. I think they also embody service in such a humble way. They need to do some of the most humbling jobs for people who are sick or incapacitated. They are a worldly expression of the care Jesus calls us to show others in need. We can learn a lot from the way nurses care for others.

When was the last time you cared for someone else like your nurses care for you? As a mother to your children or the child inside, you already know what it's like to humbly care for them. But how can you also show care to others in your life? Maybe you can't physically help others right now, but whom can you encourage, laugh with, or listen to? I imagine you are the focus of everyone's care right now, but that doesn't mean you can't also care for others right now. We are called to be the hands and feet of Jesus. Find someone to serve today with a smile or kind words— maybe one of your nurses.

L I S T E N

"I Will Carry You" by Michael W. Smith
"If We Are the Body" by Casting Crowns

Bed Rest Survival Tip

———— ℨ•℥ ————

Write thank-you cards to your nurses. God cares for you through your nurses. He has gifted them with care and nurturing. They are truly a gift from God.

A Prayer for Nurses

Lord, let them be a source of strength for patients and their families. Let them be a constant help to the providers and the other nurses with whom they work. Lord, fill them with the energy to open each day with a smile regardless of how tired they are. May they be a true sign of Your love to every person under their care.

24

Tell Me Everything Is Going to Be OK

Be strong and courageous. Do not be afraid;
do not be discouraged, for the Lord your
God will be with you wherever you go.

—JOSHUA 1:9

When I am afraid, I put my trust in you.

—PSALM 56:3

So do not fear, for I am with you; do not be dismayed, for I am your
God. I will strengthen you and help you; I will uphold you with my
righteous right hand ... For I am the Lord your God who takes hold
of your right hand and says to you, Do not fear; I will help you.

—ISAIAH 41:10, 13

Peace I leave with you; my peace I give you. I do
not give to you as the world gives. Do not let your
hearts be troubled and do not be afraid.

—JOHN 14:27

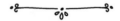

I had some fears when I was on bed rest with my triplets. I feared the usual stuff like whether I would go into labor too early, whether they would be born with some disabilities, or whether I would lose one of them. I wanted the doctors to tell me everything would be OK so I could hang on to that hope.

The fear I faced was nothing like what my friend Jamie faced. Jamie was told early on in her pregnancy that her baby had only a very small pocket of amniotic fluid, and likely the baby would be born without developed lungs. Jamie's doctors didn't give her the hope that everything would be OK; it was often the opposite. My friend sat on bed rest in constant fear of what it would be like to deliver her baby, only to watch her suffocate during her last minutes with her. However, my friend never lost her faith in God and hope that He would provide for her no matter what would come.

Jamie gave birth to a miracle. Her baby girl, Tessa, was born early but with working lungs! We praised Jesus for such a miracle. Our prayers were answered with a yes. However, even if the answer would have been a no, God promised He would have been with Jamie through the good and the bad. Sometimes we put our hope in doctors to tell us everything is going to be OK, and we trust they can make it so. Yet only God can tell us everything is going to be OK and truly mean it.

There are times when our fears do come true. The reason God calls us not to fear is because He is in control, and He will be with us no matter what trials we face. Fear robs us of the joy of living in the moment, of being brave in our faith and trusting God. If we can put away fear, we will see that no matter what comes, God is right by our side.

L I S T E N

"Fear Is a Liar" by Zach Williams
"I Will Fear No More" by The Afters
"Eye of the Storm" by Ryan Stevenson
"Hold Me Jesus" by Rich Mullins

Bed Rest Survival Tip

For this activity, you will need two sticks, some string, a bunch of flat stones you can write on, and a permanent marker. Ask a family member, friend, or nurse to bring you the items you need. Attach the sticks together, forming a cross, and wrap the center with string a few times, crossing over the sticks to hold them in place; then tie it off. Prop up your cross somewhere in your room. Now, whenever a fear is bothering you, write it down on your stone and give it to Jesus by putting it under the cross. Say a prayer and give it to God.

25

You Are Sacrificing out of Love

Whoever finds their life will lose it, and whoever
loses their life for my sake will find it.

—MATTHEW 10:39

Greater love has no one than this: to lay
down one's life for one's friends.

—JOHN 15:13

And walk in the way of love, just as Christ loved us and gave
himself up for us as a fragrant offering and sacrifice to God.

—EPHESIANS 5:2

Just as people are destined to die once, and after that to face
judgment, so Christ was sacrificed once to take away the sins
of many; and he will appear a second time, not to bear sin,
but to bring salvation to those who are waiting for him.

—HEBREWS 9:27–28

Through Jesus, therefore, let us continually offer to God
a sacrifice of praise—the fruit of lips that openly profess
his name. And do not forget to do good and to share
with others, for with such sacrifices God is pleased.

—HEBREWS 13:15–16

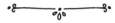

If you have kids, you already know this, but if this is your first child, you are about to learn that motherhood is sacrificing yourself for your kids—over and over. Right now you are sacrificing your normal life and activities, your body, and your sanity to take care of this baby inside you. You have begun the motherly sacrifice that will continue for years to come. You will find yourself putting your children first, in front of your own needs. You sacrifice your sleep to care for your baby. You sacrifice your money on clothes and shoes for your kids, not for you. You may sacrifice your career to stay at home and care for your kids. You sacrifice your time to drive them around to their activities just to see the smile on their faces.

Mothers know sacrifice. Jesus knows sacrifice even more. Jesus sacrificed His connection to His family. He sacrificed sleep, food, home, popularity, safety, respect, relationships, and eventually His own life to save ours. If we are to follow His example and be like Jesus, we need to be willing to sacrifice to follow God's will for our lives. If we are called to be mothers, we will be called to sacrifice.

Mothers who sacrifice their wants and desires to raise children for God's kingdom know the sacrifice is worth it. It's when we give up parts of our lives out of love for others and God that we find meaning and purpose in our lives, and we become closer to God. In this world where it's all about finding "what makes you happy" and "taking care of yourself," people are too often left feeling empty. It's when you sacrifice yourself for others that you feel fulfilled. Is the path always easy? No. But God sees your sacrifice, and He blesses it.

L I S T E N

"The Proof of Your Love" by for KING & COUNTRY
"Living Sacrifice (Live)" by Brandon Lake

Bed Rest Survival Tip

Try writing a poem about how you are making a sacrifice of love right now and how it mirrors Christ's sacrifice for you.

26

Facing Trouble

For in the day of trouble he will keep me safe in his dwelling.

—PSALM 27:5

God is our refuge and strength, an ever-present help in trouble.

—PSALM 46:1

Hear my prayer, O Lord; listen to my cry for mercy. When
I am in distress, I call to you, because you answer me.

—PSALM 86:6-7

Do not let your hearts be troubled. You
believe in God, believe also in me.

—JOHN 14:1

In this world you will have trouble. But take
heart! I have overcome the world.

—JOHN 16:33

Praise be to the God and Father of our Lord Jesus Christ, the
Father of compassion and the God of all comfort, who comforts
us in all our troubles, so that we can comfort those in any
trouble with the comfort we ourselves receive from God.

—2 CORINTHIANS 1:3-4

Is anyone among you in trouble? Let them pray.

—JAMES 5:13

When you are on bed rest, your pregnancy is at high risk. High risk means you might face trouble in your pregnancy. Each new day could present some unexpected trouble. The baby's heartbeat could be slow, you might dilate, contractions might start again, and the list goes on. I don't want to say anything more that might scare you. God already knows the troubles you are going to face while on bed rest. He already knows how this pregnancy is going to roll out. If you have already faced some troubles, they are part of God's plan, and He is carrying you through. When you read the Bible verses above, you see that God is very clear that we will face trouble in this world. But look closer ... He also said He will keep us safe; He will be our refuge, strength, ever-present help, and comfort. He doesn't leave us alone to face our troubles.

So, what does God ask from us when we face troubles? He says to trust Him and pray. We need to do only those two things. Are you facing troubles right now? Stop reading right now, pray, and trust God. Trusting Him means that even if you lose this baby, you believe God is still good. Even if your baby is born with troubles, God is still good. Trust that God has a plan and loves both of you.

L I S T E N

"God Is Good" by Jonathan McReynolds
"For the Good" by Riley Clemmons
"Yes I Will" by Vertical Worship

Bed Rest Survival Tip

———— ❧ · ❧ ————

It's easy to think of God as good when our lives are good. But faith means we believe God is good all the time—even amid our troubles. While listening to the suggested songs listed, color the next page and hang it in your room as a reminder.

27

Praying for a Big Ask

In her deep anguish Hannah prayed to the Lord, weeping
bitterly ... Hannah was praying in her heart, and her
lips were moving but her voice was not heard.

—1 SAMUEL 1:10, 13

Oh, that I might have my request, that
God would grant what I hope for.

—JOB 6:8

If you believe, you will receive whatever you ask for in prayer.

—MATTHEW 21:22

I love the story of Hannah because I identified with her—being
barren for a time and praying for God to give her a child. Hannah
was barren for years and years. I was only struggling to get
pregnant for two years, but it was still hard when others around
me got pregnant and I worried I never would. What I love about
Hannah is that she never stopped asking. She was well along in
age, and she still went to the temple to pray to God, believing He
could and would give her a child.

What big ask do you have for God? It can be easy to give up and stop praying when our prayers aren't answered right away or when doctors tell us there is no way. Sometimes it feels like God has already said no to our prayers before we really know for sure. When we read verses like Matthew 21:22, it's hard to understand what Jesus is saying, because we don't always get a yes answer to our prayers. Jesus isn't saying we will always get what we want. But when praying, the first step is to actually believe God *can* do whatever we are asking. Just by asking, we are showing God that we know He is in control, and we trust His plan. If what we are asking is part of God's plan and we ask and believe, we will receive.

Don't stop asking God for your heart's desire in prayer. Sometimes it feels burdensome to keep asking the same thing day in and day out. I'm sure Hannah felt that way. Sometimes you might need to ask a family member or friend to intercede in prayer for you for a time. But keep believing and trusting in God's perfect plan, timing, and answer. Believe God can do miracles for you.

L I S T E N

"Broken Hallelujah" by The Afters
"No Impossible with You" by I Am They
"When We Pray" by Tauren Wells

Bed Rest Survival Tip

———— 8•8 ————

What is your big ask? What is your prayer that seems impossible? I challenge you to turn that into your Hannah prayer. Pray, believing in your heart that God will answer your prayer. Share your Hannah prayer with family and friends and ask them to pray it for you too.

28

Hope and Trust Cast Out Fear

I remain confident of this: I will see the goodness
of the Lord in the land of the living.
—PSALM 27:13

Yes, my soul, find rest in God; my hope comes from him.
—PSALM 62:5

As for me, I will always have hope; I will praise you more and more.
—PSALM 71:14

May the God of hope fill you with all joy and peace
as you trust in him, so that you may overflow
with hope by the power of the Holy Spirit.
—ROMANS 15:13

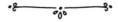

When I was trying to get pregnant, I tried to hold on to hope that my dreams and desires would be fulfilled. Once when I thought I might be pregnant, my husband said, "I just don't want you to get your hopes up, only to have them crushed." Of course, he said this in a desire to protect my feelings, but I remember thinking, *But I thought hope was a good thing.*

In the Bible, God often asks us to have hope. Hope *is* a good thing. We are called to have hope in the Lord and trust Him. Fear and hope are opposites. Somewhere I once read that hope is the desire and expectation for something to happen. Fear is the desire for something *not* to happen. I've never thought of hope as the opposite of fear before, but it makes sense. Not only is God telling us time and again to have hope, but He is also telling us not to fear.

Only God can give us hope and take away fear because He knows the whole plan. He knows what hopes will be fulfilled and what hopes will not. However, they are all part of His perfect plan for our lives. He doesn't want us to give up hope because then we invite in fear, and we no longer trust in Him and His plans for us. Hope not only keeps us from fear but also sustains us during our trials like infertility, pregnancy, and bed rest. What will you choose today—hope or fear? Yes, your hopes may not be realized, but remember, Jesus is the Hope of the world, and that Hope has already been fulfilled. It surpasses all our hopes and dreams.

L I S T E N

"Trust in You" by Lauren Daigle
"You Are My Hope" by Skillet
"Living Hope" by Phil Wickham

Bed Rest Survival Tip

———— ⚄•⚄ ————

Don't search the internet about high-risk pregnancies, premature deliveries, and so forth. You may think you want to be informed, but usually reading about these topics just creates more anxiety and fear—which you don't need. Instead, search only for success stories. Find stories of women and babies who overcame.

29
Food and Hunger

I will be fully satisfied as with the richest of foods.

—PSALM 63:5

Blessed are those who hunger and thirst for
righteousness, for they will be filled.

—MATTHEW 5:6

Do not work for food that spoils, but for food that endures
to eternal life, which the Son of Man will give you.

—JOHN 6:27

But food does not bring us near to God, we are no
worse if we do not eat, and no better if we do.

—1 CORINTHIANS 8:8

I know what it is to be in need, and I know what it is to have
plenty. I have learned the secret of being content in any and every
situation, whether well fed or hungry, whether living in plenty
or in want. I can do all this through him who gives me strength.

—PHILIPPIANS 4:12-13

Food takes on a new meaning when you are pregnant. In the first trimester for some women, the smell and thought of food make them ill. Others crave the strangest of foods. Some women are hungry all the time and can't get enough food. By the third trimester, trying to fit food in a cramped abdomen can get difficult; the heartburn starts, and the appetite is lost. Over nine months, you can go through all these different relationships with food. I was pregnant with triplets, so at times I was very sick and hated food. Later, I craved citrus fruits and nectarines. Also, I had to pack in a three-thousand-calories-a day diet when there was no room in my stomach. It felt like a constant cycle of hunger, pain, and loss of appetite.

It's strange to think about how humans have such a relationship with food. We need it to live, crave it (especially chocolate), and use it as a way to celebrate and connect with others. God knew food played an important part in our lives because He created it that way. That's why He uses it as a metaphor for a human need so often in the Bible. He equates our need for food with our spiritual hunger or need for Him.

Spiritual food is important; it's a way to connect with both God and others, and we need it for fuel to survive in this world. But what is spiritual food? It is time spent worshipping God, talking with Him in prayer, reading the Bible, talking with others about God, and serving God and others. These activities feed us spiritually and bring us closer to God. We use physical food as a way to celebrate and connect with others. Spiritual food is a way to celebrate God's goodness and connect with Him. Are you getting enough spiritual food in your diet? Are you starving your soul or filling it?

L I S T E N

"Hunger" by CeCe Winans
"Hungry (Falling on My Knees)" by Vineyard
Worship (featuring Kathryn Scott)

Bed Rest Survival Tip

———— ✦ ————

Ask a friend or family member to set up a meal sign-up so
people can make meals for your family while you are unable.
If you have children and they are picky, make sure to include a
list of family likes, dislikes, and allergies. SignUpGenius.com or
TakeThemaMeal.com are great online tools for scheduling such
a thing.

30
Friendships

A friend loves at all times.
—PROVERBS 17:17

*For I was hungry and you gave me something to eat, I was thirsty
and you gave me something to drink, I was a stranger and you
invited me in, I needed clothes and you clothed me, I was sick and
you looked after me, I was in prison and you came to visit me.*
—MATTHEW 25:35–36

*But, brothers and sisters, when we were orphaned by being
separated from you for a short time (in person, not in thought),
out of our intense longing we made every effort to see you.*
—1 THESSALONIANS 2:17

Visits from friends were the best thing ever when I was on bed
rest. There were some days when I didn't want visitors, and I really
didn't want them in the morning, but evening visitors were my
favorite thing. I missed seeing people. Friends came and brought
me fast food or desserts to eat with them. Sometimes we played
games or watched a movie together, or they painted my nails. It was
so good just to talk about what was going on in the outside world.

God puts friends in our lives so He can show His love and comfort through them. God created us as relational beings, and friends are a gift from Him. Jesus had many friends when He was on earth. He prayed with His friends, ate with them, and laughed and cried with them.

Sometimes our friends are busy, and they don't visit as often as we would like. Try not to get discouraged. It's OK to reach out and call them if you need to talk. And always remember that Jesus is your friend too, and He is right there, waiting to hear from you when you need to talk.

Also, remember what it's like to need a caring friend and take that into your future when you are off bed rest. Like Matthew 25:35–36 says, you can be the hands and feet of Jesus to others in need someday. Show God's love through your friendships.

L I S T E N

"Friend Medley" by Anthem Lights
"Brother" by NEEDTOBREATHE

Bed Rest Survival Tip

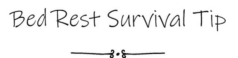

Make a guestbook or wall poster where friends who visit you can write messages to encourage you. You can keep it as a record of your visitors.

31

I Can't Get Comfortable!

May your unfailing love be my comfort,
according to your promise to your servant.
—PSALM 119:76

Shout for joy, you heavens; rejoice, you earth; burst into
song, you mountains! For the Lord comforts his people
and will have compassion on his afflicted ones.
—ISAIAH 49:13

As a mother comforts her child, so will I comfort you.
—ISAIAH 66:13

Getting physically comfortable when you are pregnant is a constant challenge, especially when confined to a bed or sofa. When I was first put on bed rest, my belly was growing so fast with triplets that my skin itched terribly all day and night from the stretching. It drove me crazy. Then my butt got sore from sitting on it all day with extra weight in a hospital bed.

Physical comfort is one thing, but then there is mental comfort.

When you are dealing with a high-risk pregnancy, sometimes it's hard for your mind to be comforted. Friends and family tell you it's all going to be OK to keep you positive. However, deep down you aren't always comforted. How do *they* know?

The truth is, God is our only comfort in life and death. His love and protection are the comfort our hearts desire. His compassion for us when we are afflicted, ailing, distressed, and uncomfortable is what we need for our bodies, minds, and souls. I love Isaiah 66:13 because I can imagine the comfort I have given my daughters over the years. I cradled them when they were upset newborns. I hugged and rocked them when they fell and hit their heads. I loved them with such nurturing care. God cares for us in the same way. He comforts us and is able to say, "It's all going to be OK," because it will be. Maybe not right away, but because of Jesus, it will be.

L I S T E N

"Abide with Me" by Audrey Assad
"Oh, the Deep, Deep Love of Jesus" by Audrey Assad

Bed Rest Survival Tip

Comfort Tips:

- Change your position often to relieve pressure from your bum.

- If you are allowed, move from the bed to a chair for a while.
- Adjust pillows often to give you the best support.
- If you're in the hospital, ask the nurses to make your bed every morning for you if possible—wrinkly sheets are the worst (if you are home, ask a loved one).
- Ask for clean sheets while you take a shower.
- Ask someone to bring you an extremely comfortable outfit, pajamas, and/or robe.
- Ask someone to bring your favorite comfort foods.
- When you cry, imagine God rocking you and telling you it's going to be OK.

32
Let Go and Let God

The Lord will fight for you; you need only to be still.
—EXODUS 14:14

If only you would be altogether silent!
For you that would be wisdom.
—JOB 13:5

Are you so foolish? After beginning by means of the Spirit,
are you now trying to finish by means of the flesh?
—GALATIANS 3:3

May the God of peace ... equip you with everything
good for doing his will, and may he work in us
what is pleasing to him, through Jesus Christ.
—HEBREWS 13:20-21

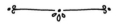

Sitting still … on bed rest, you know how hard and boring that can be. We are active creatures, and God created us that way. We like to do things like create, move, travel, fix, and play. However, there are times in our lives when we just need to be still, let go, and let God do it for us. Bed rest is one of those times. All we can do is just be still and let God take care of the life or lives within us. It is so much better to let go of the stress and worry of trying to do everything ourselves and just let God take care of it for us because—let's be honest—He is taking care of it all anyway.

The other great thing about being still is that when you are quiet and the world slows down, you are able to listen for God's voice, feel His comfort, and see His guidance. It's hard for us to be still these days in such a fast-paced world, but it is in forced stillness that we are blessed.

You might be weighed down with all the things you should be doing at home, at work, and for your family. Today, give those matters up to God in prayer, let go of them, and be still. If something needs to be done, He will do it. If He doesn't do it, it doesn't need to be done. How comforting is that?

L I S T E N

"Be Still" by Hillsong Live
"Be Still My Soul" by Kari Jobe

Bed Rest Survival Tip

Create a list titled "I will be still and let God take care of it for me." Then anytime you have something you are worried you aren't doing (at home, at work, for friends or family, for yourself), write it down on the list. Hang your list in your room somewhere or keep it near so you can keep adding to it. When God takes care of the item for you, cross it off.

33
Shine Your Light

May those who fear you rejoice when they see
me, for I have put my hope in your word.
—PSALM 119:74

In the same way, let your light shine before others, that they
may see your good deeds and glorify your Father in heaven.
—MATTHEW 5:16

Do nothing out of selfish ambition or vain conceit. Rather in
humility value others above yourselves, not looking to your
own interests but each of you to the interests of the others.
—PHILIPPIANS 2:3-4

Therefore, as God's chosen people, holy and dearly
loved, clothe yourselves with compassion, kindness,
humility, gentleness and patience.
—COLOSSIANS 3:12

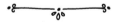

When you lie in bed all day and others cater to your needs, it's easy
to become self-involved. Everything revolves around you and your
baby. It's easy to forget about others when you are working so hard
at staying sane and caring for your unborn baby. However, even
when you are on bed rest, you have an effect on others.

I lived in the hospital for eight weeks before giving birth to my triplets. I didn't realize it then, but my attitude, my compassion for the nurses serving me, had a huge effect on them. Just because I was the patient didn't mean I had a free pass to take out my negative feelings on those around me. Instead, I chose to reflect the love of Christ.

It isn't easy to think about sharing the love of Christ when you are in a challenging situation, but it can be such a great way to witness. If you clothe yourself with compassion, kindness, humility, gentleness, and patience, then those around you will truly see the light of Christ shining from you in challenging circumstances. They will wonder where your strength comes from. Let them know where you get your strength and positive outlook.

L I S T E N

"Lights Shine Bright" by TobyMac
"Shine a Light" by Elevation Worship

Bed Rest Survival Tip

If you have wheelchair privileges, visit other moms on bed rest and encourage them. Let them see the joy and contentment of the Lord inside you. You know what they are going through. Hang encouraging Bible verses in your room. They will serve as an encouragement to you on difficult days, but you also never know who else will read them when they visit you. Set a goal to visit moms on bed rest someday when your bed rest is done.

34
I'm So Bored

So God created mankind in his own image, in the image of
God he created them; male and female he created them.
—GENESIS 1:27

May the favor of the Lord our God rest on us; establish the work
of our hands for us—yes, establish the work of our hands.
—PSALM 90:17

This is the day the Lord has made; let us rejoice and be glad in it.
—PSALM 118:24

Whatever your hand finds to do, do it with all your might,
for in the realm of the dead, where you are going, there is
neither working nor planning nor knowledge nor wisdom.
—ECCLESIASTES 9:10

Whatever you do, work at it with all your heart, as
working for the Lord, not for human masters.
—COLOSSIANS 3:23

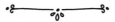

I get bored easily. I get sick of the same old, and I crave something
different. I have a hard time finishing a box of cereal because

I get sick of eating that flavor. I get bored watching TV, so I shop on my phone while watching a show that is moving along too slowly for me. I even get bored with the same songs played on the radio day after day. In this age of constant change and stimulation, we get bored easily. But bed rest brings boredom to a whole new level.

Bed rest boredom is the real deal. You get sick of watching TV, reading books, and looking at the same walls and scenery. The monotony of your days can wear on you. You just want to get up and do something different.

Do you ever wonder why we get bored? Why do we crave change and different experiences? Maybe it's because God created us to do, work, create, and explore His creation—not just exist. God created us with creative minds that love to think, solve, imagine, and compose. God gave us these gifts so we can use them and bring Him glory. So it makes sense that it doesn't feel right when we aren't using those gifts.

The good news is that you aren't limited in your creativity when on bed rest. It may feel like it, but really, when we are bored, we just aren't *using* our creativity to think of something we *can* do. Some say creativity is born out of boredom. When my brother and I were bored, my mom sent us outside. It was in our boredom that we imagined we were *Little House on the Prairie* characters, living by the creek that went through our backyard.

My ability to beat bed rest boredom with God's help was one of the reasons I was inspired to write this devotional. I wanted to provide you with daily worship and give you a variety of things to do while on bed rest. I wanted to help you get out of boredom and into God's Word for inspiration, comfort, and encouragement. I wanted to provide you with activities you could do while on bed rest. You may still get bored sometimes—and that is completely normal and OK—but the next time you feel bored, try to tap into your God-given creative side. We all have it.

L I  S T E N

"The Giving" by Michael W. Smith
"Simple Gifts (Live)" by Jim Brickman

Bed Rest Survival Tip

Stimulate your creative side. Work on crafts, knit, do scrapbooking, or draw. Play board games with your visitors. Solve brainteasers or sudoku puzzles. If you have kids, get out the Play-Doh and have fun with them. Play the suggested songs in the background.

35

I Feel like a Useless Blob!

For I was hungry and you gave me something to eat, I was thirsty and you gave me something to drink, I was a stranger and you invited me in, I needed clothes and you clothed me, I was sick and you looked after me, I was in prison and you came to visit me … Truly I tell you, whatever you did for one of the least of these brothers and sisters of mine, you did for me.

—MATTHEW 25:35-36, 40

Husbands ought to love their wives as their own bodies. He who loves his wife loves himself. After all, no one ever hated their own body, but they feed and care for their body, just as Christ does the church.

—EPHESIANS 5:28-29

Each of you should use whatever gift you have received to serve others, as faithful stewards of God's grace in its various forms.

—1 PETER 4:10

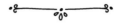

When you sit in your bed or on the sofa day after day, you begin to feel helpless and like a burden to others. It's normal to feel this way. We like doing things for ourselves. We don't like asking for help, because that means we are "weak." We want to appear strong, and we have this inner sinfulness that wants to be independent, self-sufficient, and not needing anyone—including God.

You've probably never thought about it that way, that by trying to be entirely independent and self-sufficient, you are acting like you don't need God. But think about it for a minute. God calls us to serve others so we are serving Him. If we deny others the opportunity to serve us when we are in need, we deny them the opportunity to serve God, and we deny God the opportunity to care for us through others.

You will likely experience people offering to help you while on bed rest and possibly afterward. Offering to help you out is the only way many people can think to show you love. Let God care for you through the service of others. We are created to need others and God. Put away your pride and independence, and let others help you. You aren't a burden—you are loved. Soon enough it will be your turn to serve others.

L I S T E N

"I Will Be Here" by Steven Curtis Chapman

Bed Rest Survival Tip

When others offer to help, it's easy to say, "Thank you," and never take them up on their offer because you cannot even begin to think about what you would ask from them. I suggest being prepared.

Keep a running list of what you need help with now and might need help with in the future. This way, when someone asks you whether he or she can help, you can share a need you have. This will make the person so happy to be able to help, and it will help ease your burden as well.

36

The Bills Keep Coming

The Lord will guide you always; he will satisfy your needs in a sun-scorched land and will strengthen your frame. You will be like a well-watered garden, like a spring whose waters never fail.

—ISAIAH 58:11

And my God will meet all your needs according to the riches of his glory in Christ Jesus.

—PHILIPPIANS 4:19

Keep your lives free from the love of money and be content with what you have, because God has said, "Never will I leave you; never will I forsake you."

—HEBREWS 13:5

Bed rest is financially stressful. Possibly, you used to work and can't now that you lie in bed. Maybe you have children, and your spouse needs to take more time off from work to care for them because you are unable. You may possibly need to pay for more childcare. You also may see medical bill after medical bill pile up. It's easy to fall into stress and fear about such things, but God will provide what you need.

Years after I had my triplets, I was visiting my brother and his wife in the hospital after they had a baby. I felt the Spirit poke me to go see whether any triplet moms were on bed rest there. I was introduced to a woman who was pregnant with triplets and living on government financial assistance. I began to care for and mentor this woman, who was about to give birth. She didn't have cribs, car seats, or many baby essentials. I contacted a nearby church that had a ministry; the people there lent out cribs and other large baby items. I got my girlfriends together, and we held a baby shower for this woman, giving her new and gently used items. My church also gave me money to buy her some car seats. God used me to provide for this woman's needs. Will He not provide for yours?

You may need to pare down and live with less. You may need to create a budget. You may need to ask for help and let others help you, but God will provide for your needs. If you have a particular financial stress on your mind, pray right now for God to provide and give the matter over to Him. You need to focus on staying positive and stress free for your baby.

L I S T E N

"Situation" by Jonathan McReynolds
"Do Not Worry" by Ellie Holcomb

Bed Rest Survival Tip

——— ᘉ•ᘈ ———

If you aren't working because of bed rest and are missing your income, don't be afraid to ask your church family to help with groceries, house cleaning, or gas cards for doctor office visits. This isn't charity; it is the body of Christ helping others when they need it. If you don't have a church family, ask your doctor or nurse about meeting with a social worker who can help you.

37

Why Even Ask?

Listen to my words, Lord, consider my lament. Hear my
cry for help, my King and my God, for to you I pray. In
the morning, Lord, you hear my voice; in the morning
I lay my requests before you and wait expectantly.

—PSALM 5:1–3

You, Lord, hear the desire of the afflicted; you
encourage them, and you listen to their cry.

—PSALM 10:17

I love the Lord, for he heard my voice; he heard my cry for mercy.
Because he turned his ear to me, I will call on him as long as I live.

—PSALM 116:1–2

The Lord is near to all who call on him,
to all who call on him in truth.

—PSALM 145:18

Call to me and I will answer you and tell you great
and unsearchable things you do not know.

—JEREMIAH 33:3

If you remain in me and my words remain in you, ask
whatever you wish, and it will be done for you.

—JOHN 15:7

STACEY PYLMAN

And if we know that he hears us—whatever we ask—
we know that we have what we asked of him.

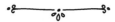

—1 JOHN 5:15

With all the major things going on in the world, like starvation, murder, hurricanes, corruption, disease, pollution, and human trafficking, why would God hear or pay attention to our small asks? Why would He care about your next ultrasound and hear your prayer for everything to be OK when a child dies from hunger every ten seconds? Why even ask God for anything when He will do what He wants anyway?

These are all very good questions and not easy to answer. What we do know is that God tells us in the Bible over and over that He hears us and wants us to keep asking Him. He wants us to talk with Him, to ask Him for things big and small, because doing so shows our hearts are trusting Him. He may answer yes. He may answer no. He may answer not yet. No matter the answer, He still wants us to ask. It is when our desires align with God's desires or plans for us that He answers yes. If our desires aren't in alignment, we may get a no. However, if we ask in humility, in a way that truly seeks to desire what God desires, He will help us change our desires and asks. We should never stop asking though because God hears us, and He cares.

L I S T E N

"Hear My Prayer" by E. Dewey Smith,
Jr. & the Hope Mass Choir
"God Hears" by Newsong
"On My Knees" by Jaci Valesquez or Nicole C. Mullen

Bed Rest Survival Tip

—— ❧•❧ ——

Ask for a good-smelling candle to brighten your day. If you are on bed rest at home, light a candle when you pray and ask God for your desires. Watch the smoke rise from the flame. Imagine that the smoke going up is your prayer going to Him.

38

Laughter Just like a Medicine

*But may the righteous be glad and rejoice before
God; may they be happy and joyful.*

—PSALM 68:3

*Our mouths were filled with laughter, our tongues
with songs of joy ... The Lord has done great
things for us, and we are filled with joy.*

—PSALM 126:2-3

A cheerful heart is good medicine.

—PROVERBS 17:22

*A time to weep and a time to laugh, a time
to mourn and a time to dance.*

—ECCLESIASTES 3:4

Did you know that laughter builds immunity, lowers your stress
hormones, decreases pain, and relaxes your muscles? What
great medicine for a pregnant woman! The days are long, and
sometimes it doesn't feel like there is much to laugh about when

you are on bed rest. But when I think back, there really were some funny times. When my nurse had to shower with me, I couldn't help but laugh with her. When my little nieces and nephews came to talk to my belly, I had to giggle. When I watched old *Seinfeld* episodes with my husband, we laughed together. When someone gave me a "Wide Load" sign, I laughed to tears.

God created us to experience joy and laughter, but He also created us to benefit from them. What a wonderful, loving God! It's not a coincidence that laughter and light heal us while stress, anger, and fear physically and emotionally break us down. Stress, anger, and fear are from sin, and laughter and joy are from the Lord.

Today I still struggle with physical and emotional effects on my body from stress, but I also try to stay positive and laugh with friends and family as much as possible. When I have a bad day, I know I need to connect with others who will brighten my day with laughter. One of my favorite movie quotes is from *Steel Magnolias*, when Dolly Parton's character, Truvy, says, "Laughter through tears is my favorite emotion," because it is so true for me. If you are having too many days filled with stress, fear, or sadness, find something or someone to make you laugh.

L I S T E N

"Laughter Just like a Medicine" by BeBe Winans
"Laugh Out Loud" by Jason Gray

Bed Rest Survival Tip

— ❦ —

Watch some of your favorite comedy movies or TV series. Read a funny book. Laugh with visitors or nurses when you can.

39
Our Good Shepherd

The Lord is my shepherd, I lack nothing. He makes me lie down
in green pastures, he leads me beside quiet waters, he refreshes
my soul. He guides me along the right paths for his name's sake.
Even though I walk through the darkest valley, I will fear no evil,
for you are with me; your rod and your staff, they comfort me.

—PSALM 23:1-4

He tends his flock like a shepherd: He gathers the
lambs in his arms and carries them close to his
heart; he gently leads those that have young.

—ISAIAH 40:11

I am the good shepherd. The good shepherd lays down his
life for the sheep ... I am the good shepherd; I know my sheep
and my sheep know me—just as the Father knows me and
I know the Father—and lay down my life for the sheep.

—JOHN 10:11, 14-15

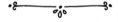

While on bed rest, one of my friends, who was also one of my
nurses at my high-risk OB-GYN, gave me three little stuffed lambs
for the babies. I propped them up on the window ledge in my

hospital room. They were a special gift. As I lay there, looking at them day after day, they inspired me to write a poem.

Little Lambs

> Each and every day I pray,
> "Lord, watch Your little lambs today.
> There's not much more that I can do
> Than fully put my trust in You.
> I patiently await the day of praise
> When You give me your lambs to raise.
> Give me strength, wisdom, and grace;
> And in my hugs, may they feel Your embrace."
> Each and every day I pray,
> "Lord, watch Your little lambs today."

The many times I heard the story of the Good Shepherd while I was growing up inspired my poem. Learning about how helpless sheep are, I realized that my babies were just as helpless and needed a protector. Jesus promised to be our protector when He told the parable of the Good Shepherd. He promised to lay down His life for the sheep, and Jesus did just that.

I worried daily about what would happen and whether all the babies would survive. I knew there really wasn't much I could do except trust God and pray. I knew that even if my babies didn't survive in this world, Jesus had already laid down His life and saved them so they would be welcomed into heaven. With that peace of mind, I then prayed that He would protect them in this world too ... so I could be their mom for a while. This time God answered yes because it was in His plan; it was His desire. Amen!

Allow Jesus to be your shepherd and your baby's shepherd. He knows you both by name, and He will be your protector. Follow His voice and let Him lead you.

L I S T E N

"Savior, like a Shepherd Lead Us" by Fernando Ortega
"Shepherd" by Crowder
"Watch over Me" by Aaron Shust

Bed Rest Survival Tip

———❧·❧———

There is a lot to be done when preparing to care for a baby. Make a list of things that still need to be done around your house and give it to family and friends to take care of for you.

40

This Is beyond What I Can Bear

You will keep in perfect peace those whose mind
is steadfast, because they trust in you.

—ISAIAH 26:3

No temptation has overtaken you except what is common to
mankind. And God is faithful; he will not let you be tempted
beyond what you can bear. But when you are tempted, he
will also provide a way out so that you can endure it.

—1 CORINTHIANS 10:13

Consider it pure joy, my brothers and sisters, whenever you face
trials of many kinds, because you know that the testing of your
faith develops perseverance. Let perseverance finish its work so
that you may be mature and complete, not lacking anything.

—JAMES 1:2-4

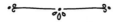

Bed rest is hard. Sitting by yourself alone, unable to get comfortable while bored, worried, and sick, isn't for the faint of heart. Your body, mind, and faith are all being challenged at the same time. It feels like God is testing you, and you are failing the test. Sometimes it feels like it is beyond what you can bear. You know what? It *is* beyond what you can bear!

When I was on bed rest, my fellow triplet mother friends gave me the most wonderful sign. It said, "God doesn't give us what we can handle; God helps us handle what we are given." My mom loved this sign and explained to me that often people misquote the verse from 1 Corinthians 10:13 by saying God won't give you what you can't handle. My wise mom said that is so wrong. Every day we are given more than we can handle alone. We have illnesses, job losses, and deaths of loved ones. In this world, we will have troubles. But the promise from God is that He will help us handle and overcome what we are given.

God is here right now, helping you handle whatever comes your way. Does He want you to suffer? No. That is just the result of sin. But God doesn't leave us alone to try to handle the sin, pain, and sadness in our lives all by ourselves. We would never be able to handle it alone. God isn't testing you to see how much you can bear alone. He might allow challenges in your life so your faith and trust in Him will grow. Keep the faith and look to God to help you bear what you are given.

L I S T E N

"Rescue" by Lauren Daigle
"Truth I'm Standing On" by Leanna Crawford
"Strong Enough" by Matthew West

Bed Rest Survival Tip

If someone would like to buy you a gift, suggest a sign that says, "God doesn't give us what we can handle; God helps us handle what we are given." Hang it in your room and read it often.

If you must go on any medications like magnesium sulfate that make you feel terrible, it's not the end of the world. It's OK to cry. Call a friend who has been in a situation like yours. Talk on the phone or ask her to come and visit you.

41

I'm So Lonely— Where Are You?

The Lord himself goes before you and will be with you; he will never leave you nor forsake you. Do not be afraid; do not be discouraged.

—DEUTERONOMY 31:8

I keep my eyes always on the Lord. With him at my right hand, I will not be shaken.

—PSALM 16:8

Turn to me and be gracious to me, for I am lonely and afflicted.

—PSALM 25:16

Yet I am always with you; you hold me by my right hand. You guide me with your counsel, and afterward you will take me into glory.

—PSALM 73:23-24

And surely I am with you always, to the very end of the age.

—MATTHEW 28:20

STACEY PYLMAN

Before bed rest, you could see your friends whenever you wanted. You could go out and experience human interaction at stores, school, work, movie theaters, and restaurants. When you are on bed rest, all this social activity comes to a halt. Now your visitors come only when they are able, and you cannot go out and visit people whenever you would like. Yes, you might still get visitors, but bed rest can be very lonely, especially at night.

At night people don't come for visits very often. They usually leave after supper. If you are used to being with a spouse, you are very aware of when he leaves for the night. Nights were hard for me because I always felt like everyone was off to do his or her normal life, and there I sat … still. Suddenly it's just you, the baby, and—if you are in a hospital—your nurses if you need them. The silence is something we aren't used to. We equate silence with loneliness.

We are lonely because we forget about our relationship with Jesus. We rely on others to fulfill our relationship needs. But it's during these quiet, lonely times that Jesus is right there next to us. It's in the stillness, the silence, that we are able to connect with Him and hear His voice. We need to talk to Him and give Him the chance to comfort us. Jesus promises to be by our side; we simply need to seek Him. We are never lonely because we have an omniscient God who is always there. Yes, you might miss your friends, your family, but Jesus has the power to fulfill all those needs if we let Him.

L I S T E N

"Look Up Child" by Lauren Daigle
"There Was Jesus" by Zach Williams and Dolly Parton
"Never Alone" by BarlowGirl
"You're Not Alone" by Meredith Andrews

Bed Rest Survival Tip

—— 8·8 ——

OK, this may sound crazy, but it really isn't. When you are lonely, imagine Jesus is sitting in a chair next to your bed, visiting with you. Talk to Him aloud just like you would to a physical friend sitting there. Tell Him about your day, your worries, and your funny stories. You will feel less lonely, and you will grow closer in your relationship with Jesus. Now is your time. No one is watching or listening. The first few times you do this, you may feel weird, but I promise you will get used to it, and it will be worth it.

42

Waiting in Hope

We wait in hope for the Lord; he is our help and our shield. In him our hearts rejoice, for we trust in his holy name. May your unfailing love rest upon us, Lord, even as we put our hope in you.

—PSALM 33:20-22

May those who fear you rejoice when they see me, for I have put my hope in your word.

—PSALM 119:74

And we know in all things God works for the good of those who love him, who have been called according to his purpose.

—ROMANS 8:28

Waiting and waiting in hope are two very different things. When someone waits without hope, the waiting becomes full of fear, anxiety, impatience, and even bitterness. Have you waited in fear and anxiety before? Waiting for a boyfriend to propose, waiting to be called in for an interview, waiting to see if you got the house you bid on, waiting to get pregnant, or waiting for a diagnosis. It's easy to let the negative emotions take over while waiting. But what good do they do?

Those who wait in hope on the Lord wait with a sense that He is in control. He works everything for good, so why do we worry about the outcome? It isn't as if everything will go perfectly according to our plans, but we can be assured that everything will work out according to God's plans.

When we let go and give control to God, we are able to wait in hope. This isn't always easy to do. My friend Jamie, who was on bed rest while carrying a baby not expected to breathe at birth, struggled with hoping because hopes can be crushed when things don't turn out how we want. However, she continued to put her hope in the Lord because only He had the power to carry out His good and perfect plans. Her baby was born breathing, and she is a living miracle to this day. Who better to put our hope in than the Lord of all, who works out everything for good?

L I S T E N

"Our Hope Endures" by Natalie Grant
"Reason" by Unspoken

Bed Rest Survival Tip

Color the hope sign on the next page or search the internet for "hope coloring pages for adults" and ask someone to print one you like. Every day while you pray, color your hope picture a little more. When you're done, hang it on your wall.

43

You May Be Weak, but He Is Strong

My flesh and my heart may fail, but God is the strength of my heart and my portion forever.
—PSALM 73:26

He said to me, "My grace is sufficient for you, for my power is made perfect in weakness." Therefore, I will boast all the more gladly about my weaknesses, so that Christ's power may rest on me. That is why, for Christ's sake, I delight in weaknesses, in insults, in hardships, in persecutions, in difficulties. For when I am weak, then I am strong.
—2 CORINTHIANS 12:9–10

To this end I strenuously contend with all the energy Christ so powerfully works in me.
—COLOSSIANS 1:29

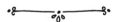

I remember thinking many times when I was on bed rest, *I have to be strong for these babies.* It's almost laughable because the longer I sat there, the weaker my body got. My body was never as weak as it was after sitting on bed rest for nine weeks. I remember after giving birth that I could barely walk down the hospital hallway. When I got home, I was fatigued after simply walking across my house. It took all the strength I could muster to visit my babies in the neonatal unit.

It was so clear to me when I was on bed rest and then as a new mother of triplets that God was going to have to be my strength. I had no physical or mental strength by the end of bed rest. My legs had withered. I was tired and overwhelmed. I was fully reliant on God to give me strength in my weakness. He gave me strength of mind to keep going.

He gives us strength when we are at our weakest. You merely need to ask in prayer for His strength and power. Will you be able to run a marathon or lift a car? Likely not, but He will give you exactly the strength you need to do what He desires. He will give you strength to do what you need to do, and if you need to do more than you are able, He will provide someone to help. Wait and see!

L I S T E N

"Stronger" by Mandisa
"Overcomer" by Mandisa

Bed Rest Survival Tip

If you are able, do some bed rest exercises. Search the internet for "pregnancy bed rest exercises" and ask your nurses about them. They can keep some of your muscles strong but also give you some mental uplift too. Pray for strength of body, mind, and soul. Watch for God's strength to show up in your weakness.

44

Mission Possible

Is anything too hard for the Lord? I will return to you at the appointed time next year, and Sarah will have a son.

—GENESIS 18:14

Ah, Sovereign Lord, you have made the heavens and the earth by your great power and outstretched arm. Nothing is too hard for you.

—JEREMIAH 32:17

For nothing is impossible with God.

—LUKE 1:37

Now to him who is able to do immeasurably more than all we ask or imagine, according to his power that is at work within us, to him be glory in the church and in Christ Jesus throughout all generations, for ever and ever! Amen!

—EPHESIANS 3:20-21

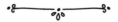

While on bed rest, you will be showered with worries and questions. *How will I be able to survive lying down for days, weeks, or even months? So many things are going wrong with this pregnancy; how will I ever make it to the end? Will they be able to stop the labor?*

Maybe you have been given grim predictions about the future of your baby, and you are praying for a miracle but secretly inside you think, *How could it ever happen?*

No matter the circumstances you face now, with God all things are possible. There is nothing too hard for Him to accomplish. He doesn't care about statistics or one problem stacking on another. He is bigger than all the problems or circumstances you face. If it is His will, He will make it happen. He is a God who moves mountains.

If you need a miracle, ask Him for it. Have faith that He can do it. He may choose not to, but He can. It is such a comfort knowing God has more power and control in His fingertip than all the amazing doctors in this world. Rest in His power and care today. Thank God for being the God of miracles.

L I S T E N

"Yes He Can" by CAIN
"Power" by Elevation Worship
"There Is Power" by Lincoln Brewster

Bed Rest Survival Tip

Write out Jeremiah 32:17 on the cover of your prayer journal or place it on a piece of paper and hang it on the ceiling above your bed. Remember to start your prayer every night by praying this verse. It will remind you of who is in control.

45

I Feel like Crying All Day

In her deep anguish Hannah prayed to the Lord, weeping bitterly.
—1 SAMUEL 1:10

You, Lord, hear the desire of the afflicted; you
encourage them, and you listen to their cry.
—PSALM 10:17

In my distress I called to the Lord; I cried to my
God for help. From his temple he heard my voice;
my cry came before him, into his ears.
—PSALM 18:6

Weeping may stay for the night, but
rejoicing comes in the morning.
—PSALM 30:5

Jesus wept.
—JOHN 11:35

In the same way, the Spirit helps us in our weakness.
We do not know what we ought to pray for, but the Spirit
himself intercedes for us through wordless groans.
—ROMANS 8:26

He will wipe every tear from their eyes. There will be no more death or mourning or crying or pain, for the old order of things has passed away.

—REVELATION 21:4

I had many sad days on bed rest. There were some mornings when I just woke up sad. I didn't really know why. Nothing had changed. But I just knew I was going to be sad that day. But you know what? God seemed to always follow up my sad days with really good days. I thought that was so merciful. He did that so I could keep going.

Feel like crying right now? Have you had a day when you wanted to cry all day? It is completely normal, especially when you are on bed rest. There is nothing wrong with crying. God Himself grieves when sad, and He calls you to cry out when you are sad and afflicted.

You might be faced with some awful news, and you don't even second-guess your reaction to cry, but what if it's lasting days upon days?

In our world we often see crying as a sign of weakness. Crying about our situations might make us feel like we aren't strong enough, like our faith isn't strong enough. But crying out to God takes strength. It takes strength to say, "I can't do this—I need You, God!"

As women we also have these wonderful hormones that mess with our emotions too. When we are pregnant, the hormones and emotions seem to be in overdrive. No wonder you feel like crying. Sometimes it feels better just to have a good cry, to let it all out. But here's the key—don't stay wallowing in misery. God wants us to cry, but He doesn't want us to stay miserable for long because then we are forgetting the hope He gives. Look to Him to bring you joy and take away your sadness. In the meantime, know He is listening to your cries and that His heart breaks with you.

L I S T E N

"Better than a Hallelujah" by Amy Grant
"Cry Out to Jesus" by Third Day

Bed Rest Survival Tip

Just cry. Let it out. It doesn't do any good to hold it inside. Cry alone, cry with your nurses, or cry with your visitors. Spend a day crying and being sad. Watch a sad movie and listen to sad songs. But tomorrow wake up new and refreshed and work hard to look at the positive.

46

Loving Someone You Haven't Met Yet

Love is patient, love is kind. It does not envy, it does not boast, it is not proud. It does not dishonor others, it is not self-seeking, it is not easily angered, it keeps no record of wrongs. Love does not delight in evil but rejoices with the truth. It always protects, always trusts, always hopes, always perseveres. Love never fails.
—1 CORINTHIANS 13:4-8

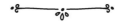

When attending weddings, you have probably heard the verses from 1 Corinthians 13 many times. You may have even heard these verses at *your* wedding. Often these verses are applied to a spouse, but love isn't just for married couples. Love described here can be for children as well. You have great love for this baby inside you. But how can you love someone you have never met? There is a life inside you. You have seen images on an ultrasound screen. You've felt the baby kick inside you. You know this child even if you haven't met him or her. Yes, you love this child you haven't met, but why? How? You love because this child is a part of you, created from you by God.

But how do you show love to a baby still in the womb? First Corinthians 13:7 tells us that love "always protects, always trusts, always hopes, always perseveres. Love never fails." As you lie on bed rest, you show the greatest love—a love that protects, trusts, hopes, and perseveres. You lie in bed even when you want to get up, because you want to protect this child. You put your hope and trust in the Lord to take care of you and your baby. You persevere in this difficult time. Why? Where does that kind of love come from? It comes from God, the One we love even though we haven't met Him face-to-face yet. Ask yourself, *If I can love my child this much, how much more does God love us with unfailing love?*

L I S T E N

"Love Never Fails" by Brandon Heath
"Drops in the Ocean" by Hawk Nelson

Bed Rest Survival Tip

Write a love letter to God. Tell God why you love him. Tell God what you are doing because of His love for you and your love for Him.

47

When God Says No

If we are thrown into the blazing furnace, the God we serve is able to deliver us from it, and he will deliver us from Your Majesty's hand. But even if he does not, we want you to know, Your Majesty, that we will not serve your gods or worship the image of gold you have set up.

—DANIEL 3:17–18

Then Jesus told his disciples a parable to show them that they should always pray and not give up.

—LUKE 18:1

Three times I pleaded with the Lord to take it away from me. But he said to me, "My grace is sufficient for you, for my power is made perfect in weakness." Therefore I will boast all the more gladly about my weaknesses, so that Christ's power may rest on me.

—2 CORINTHIANS 12:8–9

When you ask, you do not receive, because you ask with wrong motives, that you may spend what you get on your pleasures.

—JAMES 4:3

This is the confidence we have in approaching God: that if we ask anything according to his will he hears us. And if we know that he hears us— whatever we ask— we know that we have what we asked of him.

—1 JOHN 5:14–15

When you are waiting for a baby to be born, you pray a lot. You pray for the baby to be born healthy. You pray that you will be able to withstand the labor. You pray that everything will be okay with your family while you are on bed rest. God wants us to pray, and it is good that you do. But what about when God doesn't answer your prayers with the yes you desire? Some people call them "unanswered prayers." There really aren't any unanswered prayers. God always answers with yes, no, or not yet.

So, what do you do when God answers that it's not yet time? You keep praying, and you stay faithful to Him and follow His will or plan. You pray you won't get bitter. You trust that God knows what is best for you and your family.

What do you do when God answers no? You pray that you can accept His answer. You remain faithful and follow His will or plan. You pray that you won't get bitter. You trust that God knows what is best for you and your family.

Do you see how the response is the same whether God says no or not yet? One of the best things I learned when God was telling me not yet was to pray that my desires would align with His and that I would remain patient. When God tells me no, I have learned to wait and see what He desires instead, because He always has a plan.

If you are praying and haven't gotten an answer yet or did get an answer and it wasn't what you were praying for, don't give up on God. He does hear you. Pray that your desires will align with His and that you won't grow bitter. Remind yourself that He loves you more than you know, and if it was good to give you a yes answer, He would have done so.

L I S T E N

"Even If" by MercyMe
"Even When It Hurts" by Hillsong UNITED

Bed Rest Survival Tip

Make a list of things you asked for in the past that God said no to. Then reminisce about what God gave you instead. You might be surprised that God had even better plans for you than what you wanted.

48

I Miss My Man!

Though one may be overpowered, two can defend themselves.
A cord of three strands is not quickly broken.
—ECCLESIASTES 4:12

All night long on my bed I looked for the one my heart
loves; I looked for him but did not find him.
—SONG OF SONGS 3:1

His mouth is sweetness itself; he is altogether
lovely. This is my beloved, this is my friend.
—SONG OF SONGS 5:16

Love is patient, love is kind ... It always protects, always
trusts, always hopes, always perseveres. Love never fails.
—1 CORINTHIANS 13:4, 7-8

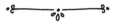

I realize some of you might not be married or even have a significant other right now, so if you don't, feel free to skip this devotion. For those of you who do have a partner right now, you might start to really miss him. I missed my husband when I was on bed rest. Because of his hyperactivity, he irritated me when he came to visit. He would press all the buttons on my hospital bed, he would shift uncomfortably in the hospital chair, and he would simply look bored sometimes. I couldn't handle the irritation, so I limited him to visiting me only three times a week at the hospital. (I was blessed enough to have friends and family close by who filled in the gaps.) But I still missed him when he wasn't there. I missed our date nights and any sort of romance.

Romantic love is a gift from God. When we experience it, especially with a spouse, it is hard to go without it for a while. Our romantic relationships need quality time, and right now you have all the time in the world. However, your partner might not have the same amount of time to give to you, so you might feel an imbalance.

God designed marriage, and it is a good thing, but because of this sinful and broken world, keeping a marriage strong takes work. Even though you are on bed rest, keep working on connecting with your partner. Love your partner "in sickness and in health." Remember, God is part of your cord keeping you together. Pray that your marriage makes it through the stress of bed rest and a new baby. Pray for your partner too. Yes, bed rest is hard for you—but it's hard for him too!

L I S T E N

"God Gave Me You" by Dave Barnes

Bed Rest Survival Tip

———— ❧ ————

Plan a date night. Put on makeup and get a friend to do your hair. Sip sparkling cider. Light LED candles and have a candlelight dinner. Watch a movie and snuggle. Reminisce about good times.

49

I'm Sick and Tired
of the Same!

The Lord said to Moses, "I will rain down bread
from heaven for you. The people are to go out each
day and gather enough food for that day."

—EXODUS 16:4

The rabble with them began to crave other food, and again the
Israelites started wailing and said, "If only we had meat to
eat! We remember the fish we ate in Egypt at no cost— also the
cucumbers, melons, leeks, onions and garlic. But now we have
lost our appetite; we never see anything but this manna!"

—NUMBERS 11:4-6

He humbled you, causing you to hunger and then feeding
you with manna, which neither you nor your ancestors had
known, to teach you that man does not live on bread alone
but on every word that comes from the mouth of the Lord.

—DEUTERONOMY 8:3

That very day, they ate some of the produce of the land: unleavened
bread and roasted grain. The manna stopped the day after they
ate this food from the land; there was no longer any manna for
the Israelites, but that year they ate the produce of Canaan.

—JOSHUA 5:11-12

But if we have food and clothing, we
will be content with that.

—1 TIMOTHY 6:8

I can still smell it—the scent of the covered hospital food tray. A gross odor of hot plastic and a mix of food scents. I was so grateful I didn't have to make any food, and I was being served while on bed rest, but I was getting sick of the same cafeteria food choices. The only thing that ever sounded good was the chocolate cake. I was fortunate that the hospital where I lived had some other restaurants in it, and I could order some better stuff from their menus sometimes. However, I needed to learn to be content and grateful for what I had. My nightly delivery of peanut butter and jelly toast and chocolate milk at nine p.m. also helped.

As someone who grew up in the United States, I have been extremely blessed with an overabundance of food. I have been spoiled with tons of food choices, and I can usually get it when I want. Living on bed rest and being more limited took some adjustment. It's so funny how we can become discontent so fast, even when we are being cared for so well. Just like the Israelites who were provided manna from heaven, I was grumbling that I was sick of that hospital food. I craved what I couldn't have instead of being grateful for what I did have.

Contentment is hard for humans. We are constantly tempted to want what we don't have instead of recognizing what we do have. It's common to yearn for more, but it's good to work on contentment and thanking God for all He provides for us.

L I S T E N

"Only Jesus" by Brian Johnson
"All I Need Is You" by Lecrae
"I Shall Not Want" by Audrey Assad

Bed Rest Survival Tip

Sick and tired of hospital food or casseroles? Ask a friend to bring you some of your favorite takeout.

50
I'm So Human, and They'll See!

The Lord does not look at the things people look at. People look
at the outward appearance, but the Lord looks at the heart.
—1 SAMUEL 16:7

Those who look to him are radiant; their
faces are never covered with shame.
—PSALM 34:5

As water reflects a face, so one's life reflects the heart.
—PROVERBS 27:19

Charm is deceptive, and beauty is fleeting; but a
woman who fears the Lord is to be praised.
—PROVERBS 31:30

I the Lord search the heart and examine the mind,
to reward each person according to their conduct,
according to what their deeds deserve.
—JEREMIAH 17:10

Your beauty should not come from outward adornment,
such as elaborate hairstyles and the wearing of gold
jewelry and fine clothes. Rather, it should be that of

your inner self, the unfading beauty of a gentle and quiet spirit, which is of great worth in God's sight.

—1 PETER 3:3-4

Knock, knock. Who's there? No, this isn't a joke. One of the unexpected outcomes of being on bed rest in the hospital is that visitors can come whenever it works for them. That means you might have unexpected visitors in the morning—like just after you wake up when your hair is disheveled, you haven't even brushed your teeth, and you don't have a bra on! One morning I was in the middle of eating my hospital breakfast when nature called. I was sitting in the bathroom, waiting to have my "morning constitutional," when a nurse knocked on the door and said there was a man there to visit me. What? I was totally not ready for a visitor and definitely not a man. I told the nurse to have him wait in the lounge room until I was done—you know—and I scrambled to find a bra to put on. It turned out it was a nice older gentleman from my church, and he was there to give me some baked goods and visit. Luckily, he didn't stay long.

The thing most people don't realize is that visiting someone who is on bed rest is like visiting someone in her bedroom in the morning. It's quite awkward! How many people would knock on someone's bedroom door at eight a.m. without calling first to make sure he or she was up and ready for visitors? Well, when you are in the hospital, apparently it doesn't matter.

I think the hardest thing for me was that I was one of those people who didn't leave the house without makeup on and my hair done. I always gave the image of being put together. Now here I was in my pajamas, sporting crazy hair, and wearing no makeup—and people were coming into my room! They were going to see me in all my natural glory. I mean, what is more human than having to use the bathroom? They were going to see my humanity, not the image I wanted to portray. I had to learn to let that go. People didn't care how I looked; they just wanted to be there for me. God also doesn't care how we look. He knows how human we are, and He created us that way. He doesn't look at the outside appearance. He looks at our hearts. It's when we are truly ourselves and not wearing the masks we present to the outside world that we are actually more genuine, more real. To this day, I still like to wear makeup and style my hair, but I care about it less when people see me undone, because I know where my true beauty lies—in my loving and serving heart from God.

L I S T E N

"Human Condition" by Unspoken
"Truth Be Told" by Matthew West
"Human" by Holly Starr (featuring Matthew Parker)

Bed Rest Survival Tip

If you aren't feeling well, it's OK to tell people you aren't up for visitors. If you need to use the bathroom for a while, it's OK to ask them to leave. (Who wants to go do that with someone waiting just outside the door?) It's OK to let people know you don't want visitors before or after a certain time.

51
His Mercies Are New Every Morning

You, Lord, are forgiving and good, abounding
in love to all who call to you.

—PSALM 86:5

Because of the Lord's great love we are not consumed,
for his compassions never fail. They are new every
morning; great is your faithfulness.

—LAMENTATIONS 3:22–23

The Lord within her is righteous; he does no
wrong. Morning by morning he dispenses his
justice, and every new day he does not fail.

—ZEPHANIAH 3:5

But for you who revere my name, the sun of
righteousness will rise with healing in its rays. And
you will go out and frolic like well-fed calves.

—MALACHI 4:2

Therefore we do not lose heart. Though outwardly we are wasting
away, yet inwardly we are being renewed day by day.

—2 CORINTHIANS 4:16

STACEY PYLMAN

Babies can be difficult. They can keep us up at night, crying. We can get so frustrated with them. Sometimes we just need to walk away for a bit. One day I was so done with my three one-year-olds that I just had to sit in my minivan in the garage and cry. But there was always something about going into their room the morning after a difficult day. When they saw me for the first time that day and smiled, my heart melted, and my mercies were new.

Bed rest is also hard, and you might have bad days and nights. You might get short with your nurses or loved ones. When you wake up in the morning on bed rest, you are tempted to sigh and think, *Another day of the same.* While it is true that your days become somewhat monotonous, instead think about how each day we get to start over. We get to try to love God better, love others better, make better choices, see the good in the world instead of just the bad, forgive instead of hold grudges, spread joy instead of crabbiness, and choose hope instead of fear. God's mercies are new every morning. We may have had some bad days, but we can start new. God has shown mercy and has forgiven us. When we wake up, we can smile at God, and He smiles at us, and we can start anew.

L I S T E N

"New Today" by Micah Tyler
"Joy Comes in the Morning" by Baylor Wilson
"Great Is Thy Faithfulness" by Fernando Ortega

Bed Rest Survival Tip

Every morning, open the blinds or shades and let the sunlight in. Don't sit in a dark room. The sunlight has a way of brightening your day.

52

It's All Too Much!

The Lord is close to the brokenhearted and
saves those who are crushed in spirit.

—PSALM 34:18

Cast your cares on the Lord and he will sustain you.

—PSALM 55:22

Do not be anxious about anything, but in every situation, by
prayer and petition, with thanksgiving, present your requests to
God. And the peace of God, which transcends all understanding,
will guard your hearts and your minds in Christ Jesus.

—PHILIPPIANS 4:6-7

Cast all your anxiety on him because he cares for you.

—1 PETER 5:7

*How am I ever going to make it through this? I can't lie here for
weeks, not knowing the outcome … the ending. What if I go through
all this agony and there isn't a happy ending? What if I just can't
handle bed rest anymore? What about my family back home? I'm
sure my house is falling apart.* These are just a few of the what-ifs

that run through your mind when you have all the time in the world to drown yourself in these questions. Soon you find yourself feeling overwhelmed.

God never wants us to carry all the burdens of today, tomorrow, and the future. We cannot handle anything except the present—and not even that without His help. He wants us to take all those cares, all those what-ifs, and cast them on Him. He handles all the tomorrows, so we don't need to get overwhelmed. He has it all under control. Our job is simply to trust Him, thank Him, and give our requests to Him.

Once you have given all your worries to Him, don't take the burdens of worry back again. If you leave them all with God, you will feel peace wash over you. Yes, every day there will be new what-ifs and new worries. Every day you will need to consciously give them to God and be filled with His peace again. Use your prayer time every morning to do this and be amazed at how your days change.

L I S T E N

"See the Light" by TobyMac
"Peace Be Still" by Hope Darst
"It Is Well" by Bethel Music and Kristene DiMarco

Bed Rest Survival Tip

———— ❧•❧ ————

An overwhelmed mom isn't a healthy mom. If you are overwhelmed, you are taking on too much that is out of your control. Learn to let go. Write down all the things that are overwhelming you on little pieces of paper. Then practice your shot by balling them up and throwing them in the trash can in your room. Every time you release one of these balled-up papers, imagine God is taking it from you.

53

You Gotta Have Faith

"Have faith in God," Jesus answered. "Truly I tell you, if anyone says to this mountain, 'Go, throw yourself into the sea,' and does not doubt in their heart but believes that what they say will happen. It will be done for them. Therefore I tell you, whatever you ask for in prayer, believe that you have received it, and it will be yours."

—MARK 11:22

Jesus replied, "You do not realize now what I am doing, but later you will understand."

—JOHN 13:7

Now faith is confidence in what we hope for and assurance about what we do not see.

—HEBREWS 11:1

And without faith it is impossible to please God, because anyone who comes to him must believe that he exists and that he rewards those who earnestly seek him.

—HEBREWS 11:6

Faith is believing something is true. Strong faith is certainty. Unlike hope, where you are praying for the best knowing that it might not happen, faith is having assurance or being certain something is going to happen. We often confuse the two things. We say you must have faith that you can be healed. You must have faith that the baby will be OK. We can have hope for those things, but we know that sometimes God doesn't choose to heal us, and sometimes it isn't God's plan that the baby will be OK. Faith is something more; faith is believing in God—believing He has a perfect plan and is good all the time, even when it doesn't make sense to us. Faith is believing that God cares for us and will always do what is best for us and our families. Faith is choosing God when the world tells us not to. Faith is believing the Word of God, believing Jesus died on the cross for our sins and that we will live an eternal life with God someday.

In Matthew 11:22 Jesus tells us to have faith in God in all the ways I listed above. He isn't saying that if we have enough faith in God, we can move mountains. He is saying we need to have faith in God that is as strong as that. He is saying God can move mountains, and we need to have faith that God can do anything. But if God doesn't move a mountain for you, heal you, or heal your baby, that doesn't mean you didn't have enough faith. It just means your request wasn't in God's perfect plan, and we must have faith that God's plan *is* perfect.

Having faith is hard. There will be times when your faith is shaken, and you aren't quite so certain—but don't lose your faith! Faith can be your comfort. It's hard to understand what God is doing when this world is so broken. It's hard to understand when we lose people dear to us at a young age or when everything comes crashing down around us. But having faith in God—knowing He wants the best for us, is protecting us, and has a perfect plan for our lives—gives us comfort amid the trials, pain, and suffering. Put your faith in God today.

L I S T E N

"Stand in Faith" by Danny Gokey
"We Believe" by Newsboys
"Lord I Believe in You" by Crystal Lewis

Bed Rest Survival Tip

Make a sign with Hebrews 11:1 on it. Paint it on a piece of wood or canvas with a paint marker. Recall the difference between hope and faith. Hang it in your hospital room or bedroom. When visitors ask, explain what faith means to you.

54
Miracles

He alone is your God, the only one who is worthy
of your praise, the one who has done these mighty
miracles that you have seen with your own eyes.

—DEUTERONOMY 10:21 (NLT)

But if I were you, I would appeal to God; I would lay
my cause before him. He performs wonders that cannot
be fathomed, miracles that cannot be counted.

—JOB 5:8-9

Many, Lord my God, are the wonders you have
done, the things you planned for us. None can
compare with you; were I to speak and tell of your
deeds, they would be too many to declare.

—PSALM 40:5

You are the God who performs miracles; you
display your power among the peoples.

—PSALM 77:14

Jesus replied, "What is impossible
with man is possible with God."

—LUKE 18:27

Now to him who is able to do immeasurably more than all we ask or imagine, according to his power that is at work within us, to him be glory in the church and in Christ Jesus throughout all generations, for ever and ever!

EPHESIANS 3:20-21

I tend to play it fast and loose with the word *miracle* sometimes. I find myself saying things like, "It was a miracle I made it home safe in that snowstorm!" or "What a miracle that I got that job!" What I'm really saying is, "What a blessing!" and I am thankful for those blessings. Yet blessings and miracles aren't the same things. Miracles are something special. They are defined as surprising and welcome events that aren't explicable by natural or scientific laws and are therefore considered the work of the divine—God.

I did experience a true miracle once though. I had been trying to get pregnant for two years, and it wasn't happening. I decided to see a fertility specialist about it. The doctor told me I had a blocked fallopian tube, and I wasn't ovulating every month. He said if we did nothing, we might get pregnant in the next seven years. We decided to start taking a medication called Clomid. Clomid works by stimulating an increase in the amount of hormones that support the growth and release of an egg. After I took this medication for a few weeks, they did an ultrasound and saw two good eggs in one ovary and one in the other. I asked the nurse whether this meant I could possibly have multiples, and she chuckled. She said, "No, honey. Many women have many more eggs than this and do not get pregnant at all. You only have about a five percent chance of having twins." Additionally, I had that blocked fallopian tube too.

Well, at the end of that month, I had a positive pregnancy test. I was very excited, and the bloodwork came back well. They scheduled an early ultrasound at six weeks to see what was going on. Later, I thought it was kind of strange that the doctor did the ultrasound himself, but at the time I didn't even notice. As he found the baby he said, "Here is baby A." He was lettering them! At that moment, I knew I had multiples. I was thrilled! Then he said, "And here is baby B."

I said to my husband, "Twins!" while laughing with joy. But then the doctor said, "And here is baby C."

I was shocked and said, "You have got to be kidding me! Triplets?"

The doctor responded with a chuckle. "No, ma'am, we don't kid about these things." He then explained that he had wanted to do the ultrasound himself because he hadn't seen anything like this in twenty years of his practice as a fertility specialist.

There was no good scientific explanation for triplets. I had less than a .001 percent chance of getting pregnant with triplets on Clomid due to my physical issues. Yes, this was a miracle from God!

Are you struggling with something in life and need a miracle? Not everyone gets to experience miracles in this life, but we should still pray and ask God for them. It's funny. I was often praying to get pregnant with a baby, but I would never have guessed the miracle God had in store. He was planning to bless us beyond what we would have asked or imagined. If you are struggling with something right now and need a miracle, don't be afraid to ask. God *can* do miracles. He can do things beyond our imagination, because our God is big!

L I S T E N

"Waymaker" by Mandisa
"He Still Does (Miracles)" by Hawk Nelson
"Miracles" by Colton Dixon

Bed Rest Survival Tip

—— 8·8 ——

Watch the movie *Miracles from Heaven* starring Jennifer Garner. What a great, true miracle story that will have you crying and praising God!

55

Why Don't They Understand?

You have searched me, Lord, and you know me. You know
when I sit and when I rise; you perceive my thoughts
from afar. You discern my going out and my lying
down; you are familiar with all my ways. Before a word
is on my tongue you, Lord, know it completely.

—PSALM 139:1-4

Trust in the Lord with all your heart and lean not on
your own understanding; in all your ways submit
to him, and he will make your paths straight.

—PROVERBS 3:5-6

Like one who takes away a garment on a cold day, or like vinegar
poured on a wound, is one who sings songs to a heavy heart.

—PROVERBS 25:20

Bed rest brings many visitors, and with many visitors who have
not been in your shoes, you will be privy to many awkward
comments. Because I was pregnant with triplets, I was pelted with
uncomfortable comments like, "You're pregnant with triplets? But

you don't even look pregnant!" or "Triplets? Was it natural?" or "Wow! Triplets! Better you than me!" Comments like these put you in such a strange position, unsure of how to even respond. I replied with, "Umm ... thanks?" (while thinking, *Is something wrong with my pregnancy? Should I be bigger?*) or "Yes, we naturally made them" (while thinking, *Are you seriously asking about the details of their conception?*) or simply smiled while thinking, *I'm glad it's me and not you as well.*

I love Proverbs 25:20. This simile of vinegar poured on a wound is like someone who sings songs to a heavy heart; it is just like those well-intentioned friends who say things like, "Bed rest isn't so bad. You get to sit around all day and have people wait on you!" Awkward comments like these make you want to scream through your fake smile and thinly veiled anger as you respond, "Yeah."

The thing is, no one who says these uncomfortable comments is trying to be mean or make you feel bad. Usually, these people are well intentioned or just plain curious. It's easy to get mad about these comments, but the truth is that when humans don't understand something, they are curious and often say the wrong thing. It's hard when people don't understand what you are going through. You may feel alone.

But you aren't alone. There is the One who knows all your circumstances, trials, thoughts, and fears. Like Job, you might have to ignore the commenters in your life and focus on God. God is there with you, and He understands. He will never say an awkward or inconsiderate comment, and He will laugh or cry with you when someone else does.

L I S T E N

"He Knows" by Jeremy Camp
"God Only Knows" by for KING &
COUNTRY and Dolly Parton

Bed Rest Survival Tip

———— ᔰ•ᔒ ————

Find a social media page for people on pregnancy bed rest. Share struggles and funny stories. If you are pregnant with multiples, find an area group of Mothers of Multiples (MoMs). I found a lot of help, advice, garage sale items, and laughter from my community MoMs group and Facebook site. Also share your bed rest situation with your church family. You will be surprised by how many women have been in the same boat and would love to share stories with you.

56
Home

Surely your goodness and love will follow me all the days of my life, and I will dwell in the house of the Lord forever.
—PSALM 23:6

By wisdom a house is built, and though understanding it is established; through knowledge its rooms are filled with rare and beautiful treasures.
—PROVERBS 24:3-4

Therefore everyone who hears these words of mine and puts them into practice is like a wise man who built his house on the rock. The rain came down, the streams rose, and the winds blew and beat against that house; yet it did not fall, because it had its foundation on the rock.
—MATTHEW 7:24-25

For we know that if the earthly tent we live in is destroyed, we have a building from God, an eternal house in heaven, not built by human hands. Meanwhile we groan, longing to be clothed instead with our heavenly dwelling.
—2 CORINTHIANS 5:1-2

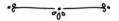

Depending on whether you are on bed rest at home or in the hospital, your view of home is different. If you are at home, you might be sick of your house and just want to get out. If you are in the hospital, you find yourself wishing for home. Isn't it funny how quickly we can become discontented? When I was in the hospital, I badly wanted to go home. There's just something about home: the comfort, the familiarity. I longed for the day I could go home with my babies. But to tell you the truth, when it was time for me to leave the hospital and go home, I had gotten used to my little hospital room: the security, the familiarity. I was nervous to go home.

That longing for home reminds me of our longing to go home to heaven. While we are here on earth, there are times when we face challenges, brokenness, pain, and sadness in this world, and we long for our heavenly home. But at the same time, when we face death, we get nervous and don't want to leave the familiar, the security of the earthly home we know. The truth is, the heavenly, eternal home God is preparing for us surpasses anything on earth, and we should be eager, thrilled, and longingly anticipate our going home to where we belong.

So what should we do now as we wait to go home? We need to build an earthly home that is built on a solid-rock foundation. That foundation or rock is Jesus. While we anticipate our heavenly home, we need to bring up our families in the Word and gospel truth so we can all reunite in our heavenly home. Our earthly homes will pass away, but our eternal home is secure.

L I S T E N

"Almost Home" by MercyMe
"Home" by Chris Tomlin

Bed Rest Survival Tip

⸻ ❧ ⸻

If you are on bed rest in the hospital, ask friends, family, or both to bring in some comforts from home like favorite blankets, photos, and toiletries. If you are stuck at home on bed rest and can't get out, go on a virtual vacation. Watch vacation videos or scroll through vacation photos. You can even research and plan your next vacation.

57

Bed Rest Is Like Waiting for Paint to Dry

Wait for the Lord; be strong and take heart and wait for the Lord.

—PSALM 27:14

Be still before the Lord and wait patiently for him.

—PSALM 37:7

I wait for the Lord, my being waits, and in his word I put my hope. I wait for the Lord more than watchmen wait for the morning, more than watchmen wait for the morning.

—PSALM 130:5-6

The end of a matter is better than its beginning, and patience is better than pride.

—ECCLESIASTES 7:8

Being strengthened with all power according to his glorious might so that you may have great endurance and patience.

—COLOSSIANS 1:11

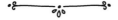

A friend once confided in me, "I think I am a patient person until I paint my nails. Why is it I always want to use my freshly painted nails?" Clearly, she wasn't patient. It's easy to say we are patient when we aren't put in situations where patience is needed. But God teaches us patience when we have to wait on Him. Patience is about accepting God's timing—accepting that we don't get to choose when our waiting is over. Once we truly give that over to God, we become patient. And once we become patient, we are no longer angry or frustrated with God.

Sitting on bed rest and waiting for the day it would be over was hard, like waiting for fingernail polish to dry times one hundred. I caught myself many times praying while on bed rest, "God, give me patience as I sit here." At thirty-three weeks pregnant, seven weeks on bed rest in the hospital, I wrote in my pregnancy journal, "I pray it is now God's time for the girls to come. If not, God, please give me patience." I didn't realize God *was* giving me patience. He was teaching me *how* to be patient. He was using my bed rest, something I had no control over, to teach me to trust Him and wait for His timing.

Now, many years later, I use that lesson of patience I learned while on bed rest and try to apply it to my everyday life.

> Me: God, when will this potty-training nightmare be over?
> God: Soon. Be patient. Your kids aren't ready yet. I have the perfect time chosen.
> Me: God, I really want to start working again.
> God: Just wait.
> Me: I really want an answer.
> God: You aren't ready for the answer yet, but I will answer you.

Do you see it? Patience isn't something you have or don't have. It's something you will need to work on constantly. Are you ready to accept God's timing and grow in your patience?

L I S T E N

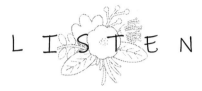

"Patient" by Apollo LTD
"Never Let You Down" Hawk Nelson

Bed Rest Survival Tip

Find someone to give you a manicure or pedicure. The pedicures are especially delightful, since you can no longer reach your toes comfortably. There's just something about getting a foot massage that makes life seem OK.

58

My Poor Body!

The Lord does not look at the things people look at. People look
at the outward appearance, but the Lord looks at the heart.

—1 SAMUEL 16:7

Charm is deceptive, and beauty is fleeting; but a
woman who fears the Lord is to be praised.

—PROVERBS 31:30

Therefore, I urge you, brothers and sisters, in view of God's
mercy, to offer your bodies as a living sacrifice, holy and
pleasing to God—this is your true and proper worship.

—ROMANS 12:1

Do you not know that your bodies are temples of the
Holy Spirit, who is in you, whom you have received
from God? You are not your own; you were bought at
a price. Therefore honor God with your bodies.

—1 CORINTHIANS 6:19-20

Pregnancy is beautiful, and I loved being pregnant (after the
morning sickness ended). I didn't mind my growing belly, even
when it was fifty inches around at the end of my pregnancy.

However, I did shed a few tears when my pregnancy was done, and I was left with what could only be described as deflated bread dough. My muscles were widely separated from the triplet pregnancy, and the skin was extremely stretched out. It recovered some, but I was left with a wrinkly reminder of how big I had gotten.

For many of us women, it's hard to look in the mirror or to step on the scale as the numbers climb. The babies cause some significant changes to our bodies. Some women take it all gracefully in stride and love that they were able to bear children, and that's a good attitude to have. Others, like me, try hard to get back to a pre-baby body.

The truth is, our bodies aren't our own; they are God's. He created us with a special purpose in His plan, and for many of us, part of that purpose is to nourish and give life to babies. It's not always a good-looking job, and we live in pajamas more than we thought we would, but it's an amazing job. We worship God by sacrificing our bodies for this plan and purpose.

God doesn't look at our stretch marks, cellulite, or sagging bums, which are the direct result of pregnancy. He looks at our beauty within: our hearts, our love for our children, and our love for Him. We are forever beautiful because we are beautiful to our Creator. Stretch marks make us more beautiful to Him because we sacrificed our bodies for the love of someone else. There is beauty in our scars.

L I S T E N

"Gold" by Britt Nicole
"Beautiful" by Bethany Dillon
"Every Bit of Lovely" by Jamie Grace

Bed Rest Survival Tip

———∽•∽———

Embrace the belly! If you have kids, let them paint on it with face paint or ask an artist friend to decorate your belly for the holidays. I've seen some amazing pumpkin and earth-painted bellies online.

59

When Will This All End?

For the revelation waits an appointed time; it speaks of the end and will not prove false. Though it linger, wait for it; it will certainly come and will not delay.

—HABAKKUK 2:3

Therefore do not worry about tomorrow, for tomorrow will worry about itself. Each day has enough trouble of its own.

—MATTHEW 6:34

Do not be anxious about anything, but in every situation, by prayer and petition, with thanksgiving, present your requests to God. And the peace of God, which transcends all understanding, will guard your hearts and your minds in Christ Jesus.

—PHILIPPIANS 4:6

Humble yourselves, therefore, under God's mighty hand, that he may lift you up in due time. Cast all your anxiety on him because he cares for you.

—1 PETER 5:6-7

One of the hardest things about bed rest is that you have plenty of time to just lie there and get anxious about when this will all end. You think about whether you will go into labor, whether it will be an emergency, whether the medications will suddenly stop working to prevent your labor, whether your delivery will be in the middle of the night or during the day, whether your spouse or loved ones will be able to make it there in time, or whether it will be too early for the baby or babies. There are so many possible scenarios as to how this is all going to end, and we have no idea how or when.

God gives us guidance in how to deal with these anxious feelings when we feel so out of control. In Philippians 4:6, He tells us not to be anxious about anything, but through prayer and thanksgiving, we should present our requests to Him. He is here and listening to our needs. When we ask Him for help and let Him work things out as he plans, His peace will come over us.

No, you don't know how this will all end. You don't know how or when. You have no control over it, and that is why you are so scared. But God knows it all. Right now, He knows exactly the day, hour, and second this baby is coming. Why? Because this is all part of His perfect plan. Put your trust in Him, and you will receive His peace.

L I S T E N

"While I'm Waiting" by John Williams
"Stay and Wait" by Hillsong UNITED

Bed Rest Survival Tip

———— 8·8 ————

When you start to get anxious and lost in a lot of what-if thoughts, escape in a book or good movie (after praying, of course). Sometimes the best solution for the stresses of this world is to give them to God and escape to a fantasy world for a little while.

60

Preparing for Arrival

Therefore keep watch, because you do not know on what day your Lord will come. But understand this: If the owner of the house had known at what time of night the thief was coming, he would have kept watch and would not have let his house be broken into. So you also must be ready, because the Son of Man will come at an hour when you do not expect him.

—MATTHEW 24:42-44

Do not let your hearts be troubled. You believe in God; believe also in me. My Father's house has many rooms; if that were not so, would I have told you that I am going there to prepare a place for you? And if I go and prepare a place for you, I will come back and take you to be with me that you also may be where I am. You know the way to the place where I am going.

—JOHN 14:1-4

Therefore put on the full armor of God, so that when the day of evil comes, you may be able to stand your ground, and after you have done everything, to stand.

—EPHESIANS 6:13

Preach the word; be prepared in season and out of season; correct, rebuke and encourage— with great patience and careful instruction ... Keep your head

in all situations, endure hardship, do the work of an
evangelist, discharge all the duties of your ministry.
—2 TIMOTHY 4:2, 5

But in your hearts revere Christ as Lord. Always be prepared to
give an answer to everyone who asks you to give the reason for
the hope that you have. But do this with gentleness and respect.
—1 PETER 3:15

Prepare as much as you can. You likely prepared for this pregnancy by taking those horse pill prenatal vitamins. You have also begun to prepare by getting the nursery ready—washing and folding baby clothes, stocking diapers, getting the crib or bassinet ready. Did you already protect the outlets? Ha! You have some time yet.

We prepare because it helps us relieve some fear. We don't know exactly what is going to happen, but if we prepare as much as we can, we won't be caught off guard. We want to prepare for situations so we won't regret later scrambling at the last minute.

We prepare for things we know are coming, but how much do we prepare for Jesus's return? You may be wondering, *How do I prepare for Jesus?* The Bible tells us to ready ourselves for temptation and trials that come before Jesus returns. Paul and Timothy talk about putting on the armor of God, listening to truth, and sharing the gospel message. Are you ready to answer those who ask you to explain how you have hope and joy during trials? Keep preparing, sharing your faith, and praying continually for Jesus's return. When Jesus returns, we will want to hear, "Well done good and faithful servant."

L I S T E N

"How Great Thou Art" by Carrie Underwood and Vince Gill
"Jesus Is Coming Back" by Jordan Feliz
"Come Jesus Come" by Stephen McWhirter

Bed Rest Survival Tip

If you don't feel prepared for this baby's arrival, make a list of things that need to be done and give it to family and friends to do for you while you are on bed rest. If they help decorate or organize the nursery, ask them to take photos and share them with you.

61

You're Welcome

She gets up while it is still night; she provides food for her family ... she watches over the affairs of her household and does not eat the bread of idleness.

—PROVERBS 31:15, 27

Whatever you do, work at it with all your heart, as working for the Lord, not for human masters, since you know that you will receive an inheritance from the Lord as a reward. It is the Lord Christ you are serving.

—COLOSSIANS 3:23-24

We were not looking for praise from people, not from you or anyone else ... Instead, we were like young children among you. Just as a nursing mother cares for her children, so we cared for you.

—1 THESSALONIANS 2:6-8

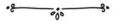

Being a mother and wife can feel like a thankless job. I often find myself saying, "You're welcome!" to my kids or husband when they don't say thank you for all the things I do for them. I like being recognized for serving others, and I like words of affirmation. Yeah, I know—I'm in the wrong line of work then. Much of what

I do as a wife and mother goes unnoticed by my family, but you know who always notices.

God sees us. He sees our service. He sees when we clean toilets, make lunches, and drive back and forth to school. He sees when we make beds, do laundry, and buy gifts for everyone. He sees when we complain while doing our work and when we do our work with joy.

Our work can seem never ending, mundane, and unappreciated, so it's important to remember who we are *really* serving. When we do our work, remembering it is for the Lord, joy in our work is returned. It is an act of service and worship to our God. We do it to show God our thanks for His mercy and saving grace in our lives. Here's a thought: when you catch yourself getting frustrated that people don't thank you for all you have done, ask yourself, "Have I thanked God today for all He has done for me?"

L I S T E N

"Do Everything" by Steven Curtis Chapman
"Breathe" by Jonny Diaz

Bed Rest Survival Tip

Read the poem "Continue On" by Roy Lessin. It is a wonderful poem about the value of a mother's life. You can find the whole poem online, but here are some excerpts:

A woman once fretted over the usefulness of her life …

At times she got discouraged because so much
of what she did seemed to go unappreciated.
"Is it worth it?" she often wondered. "Is there
something better that I could be doing with my time?"

It was during these moments of questioning that she heard
the still, small voice of her heavenly Father speak to her heart …

"What you invest in them is an offering to Me."

62

Hitting the Wall

Listen to my words, Lord, consider my lament. Hear my
cry for help, my King and my God, for to you I pray.
—PSALM 5:1-2

I am worn out from my groaning; all night long I flood
my bed with weeping and drench my couch with tears.
—PSALM 6:6

Restore to me the joy of your salvation and
grant me a willing spirit, to sustain me.
—PSALM 51:12

When my heart was grieved and my spirit embittered,
I was senseless and ignorant; I was a brute beast before
you. Yet I am always with you; you hold me by my right
hand … My flesh and my heart may fail, but God is
the strength of my heart and my portion forever.
—PSALM 73:21-23, 26

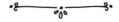

STACEY PYLMAN

There was one particular day on bed rest when I hit the wall. I woke up depressed, and I couldn't shake it. My friends were supposed to come to visit me, and I just couldn't do it. I was sad and sick of being there, and I didn't feel good. At this point, I had been in the hospital for six weeks, and I was thirty-two weeks pregnant. I just didn't think I could do it anymore. I called my mom to come and visit me, because that is the only person I wanted when I was that sad. She came to the hospital and played Yahtzee with me, and she just let me be sad.

When my doctor came in to check on me, she said, "We wondered when you were going to hit the wall, honey." She said I had done very well with staying positive for six weeks. You know what kept me positive for so long? God. We work to trust God and find joy in our trials, but sometimes we also have sad days.

David had tough days and cried out in the psalms. Sometimes as Christians we don't think we can have sad days or be depressed. Yes, we have unexplainable joy from the Lord, and we know God holds us, but it is also OK to be sad about our circumstances too.

My doctor felt bad for me, and because I was physically stable enough, she let me leave the hospital for lunch at a restaurant with my husband, mom, and dad. Oops, that was a secret—don't tell anyone she did that for me. It was the best thing she could have done for my spirit, and I'm so glad God prompted her to do that for me. God knew what I needed, and it helped me go two more weeks on bed rest.

It's OK to be honest with God and let Him know how you feel. God wants to hear from you, but don't stay in the sadness. Ask God to bring you out of the pit. Ask Him to show you joy and look for it. Find any instances of love and joy around you and hold onto them.

L I S T E N

"Your Hands" by JJ Heller
"Oh My Soul" by Casting Crowns
"Lord, I Need You" by Matt Maher

Bed Rest Survival Tip

———— ❧•❧ ————

Color the "Choose Joy" coloring page and hang it in your room.

63

Wound Healing

Lord my God, I called to you for help, and you healed me.

—PSALM 30:2

He heals the broken hearted and binds up their wounds.

—PSALM 147:3

"But I will restore you to health and heal
your wounds," declares the Lord.

—JEREMIAH 30:17

Jesus turned and saw her. "Take heart, daughter," he said, "your
faith has healed you." And the woman was healed at that moment.

—MATTHEW 9:22

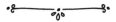

Do you have scars where your body was once cut or damaged
but now is healed? I have tons of scars from multiple surgeries.
Sometimes when I look at them, I think about how ugly they are and
how damaged my body is. But in all honesty, scars are a reminder
of the beauty of healing. Isn't it amazing how God heals our bodies?
We really don't have to do much, and a cut on our skin will heal.
That spot where you got a shot or IV will close right back up.

God heals not only our bodies from physical damage but also our hearts from emotional damage. He has the power to heal us from the inside out. Sometimes He heals us here on earth, and to Him be the glory! But the ultimate healing that will make our entire bodies and souls like new will happen when Jesus comes again and we return to heaven with Him. At that time the miracle of healing will be complete for us.

We may suffer from scars for a while on this earth, reminders of the damage we endured with God's comfort and care. But someday we will be made new with no scars, pain, or damage from sin. In heaven only Jesus will have scars. We will be given new and perfect bodies. What a day of rejoicing it will be!

L I S T E N

"Scars" by I Am They
"Scars" by TobyMac

Bed Rest Survival Tip

Take good care of your body. It is going through a lot right now. Make sure to keep it moisturized and hydrated. If you are at home, schedule an at-home massage. If you are in a hospital, ask a nurse whether there is anyone who can give you a massage.

64

Protect This Child

I am with you and will watch over you wherever you go ... I will
not leave you until I have done what I have promised you.

—GENESIS 28:15

Let the beloved of the Lord rest secure in him, for he shields him all
day long, and the one the Lord loves rests between his shoulders.

—DEUTERONOMY 33:12

But let all who take refuge in you be glad; let them ever sing
for joy. Spread your protection over them, that those who love
your name may rejoice in you. For surely, Lord, you bless the
righteous; you surround them with your favor as with a shield.

—PSALM 5:11

"Because he loves me," says the Lord, "I will rescue him; I
will protect him, for he acknowledges my name. He will
call upon me, and I will answer him; I will be with him
in trouble, I will deliver him and honor him. With long
life I will satisfy him and show him my salvation."

—PSALM 91:14-15

We are hard pressed on every side, but not crushed;
perplexed, but not in despair; persecuted, but not
abandoned; struck down, but not destroyed.

—2 CORINTHIANS 4:8

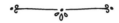

Have you ever seen a preemie in an incubator up close? The first time I saw one, I was in awe. Here was this perfect, tiny baby surviving outside the womb when really she was so tiny she couldn't live without help. That incubator was protecting her, keeping her warm when the womb no longer could. I marveled at how far we had come in science and medicine to do this for these preemies.

God protects us as we live in a world so rife with sin that we shouldn't be able to survive. He is our incubator. So many times the Bible mentions that we take refuge under His wings, like a mother bird warming her chicks. Like that incubator, He shields us from harm and keeps us safe.

I needed that reminder when I was on bed rest. Sometimes I felt like it was up to me to protect my babies and the doctors to protect me. Yes, those were our jobs, but really God was my babies' and my ultimate protector. He protects us from harm we see and harm we don't see every day.

I love Psalm 91 because at first, it sounds like God is promising protection from all harm and life without trouble, but in verse 15 He says He will be with us in trouble. In this world we will have sin and trouble, but with God protecting us, we can rest easy. Nothing can happen to us without the will of our Father in heaven. If He does allow trouble in our lives, He will be with us through it. Sleep well; you are protected, and this protection is better than any incubator we could invent.

L I S T E N

"Your Wings" by Lauren Daigle
"The Prayer" by Andrea Bocelli and Celine Dion

Bed Rest Survival Tip

If you are in a hospital, ask for a visit to the neonatal intensive care or other nurseries to see the babies. God cares for the smallest of these, and He cares for you too.

65

Isn't It OK to Be Crabby?

Refrain from anger and turn away from
wrath; do not fret— it only leads to evil.

—PSALM 37:8

Restore to me the joy of your salvation and
grant me a willing spirit, to sustain me.

—PSALM 51:12

A happy heart makes the face cheerful ... Light in a
messenger's eyes brings joy to the heart, and good
news gives health to the bones.

—PROVERBS 15:13, 30

Love is patient, love is kind ... It does not dishonor others,
it is not self-seeking, it is not easily angered.

—1 CORINTHIANS 13:4-5

Rejoice in the Lord always. I will say it again: Rejoice! Let
your gentleness be evident to all. The Lord is near ... And
the peace of God, which transcends all understanding, will
guard your hearts and your minds in Christ Jesus.

—PHILIPPIANS 4:4-5, 7

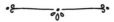

Bed rest makes you crabby. It's true. You get sick of it; you want to be doing other things, and you just get crabby. The problem with crabby is that God doesn't call us to be that way. He makes it clear that we need to fight our feelings of crabbiness, being easily angered, and fretting; instead, we should rejoice. Sounds crazy, doesn't it? How does one rejoice when he or she is living in less-than-ideal circumstances?

There is a well-known phrase out there that says, "Attitude is ten percent what happens to us and ninety percent how we respond to it." God is asking us to trust Him and stay positive because we know He is in control. A positive attitude goes a long way to improve your mental state—helping you to see the good in your situation, allowing you to see others before yourself, and making a better life for you and those around you. You see, crabbiness happens when we give in to self-centeredness and self-pity, and we want everyone around us to know we are miserable. But the Holy Spirit is within us, helping us to choose contentment over crabbiness and God and others before ourselves. Our circumstances won't change because we are crabby about them; they just make everyone miserable.

So, yes, you can feel sad and frustrated. Bring it to God. You can even share your woes with friends and family. But then you need to give it away and refuse to stay crabby. Choose positivity and contentment. Let your gentleness be evident to all. Be a positive light when others would be crabby. Ask God to take away your crabbiness so you can be a Christian light.

L I S T E N

"I Smile" by Kirk Franklin
"Trading My Sorrows" by Darrell Evans

Bed Rest Survival Tip

Invite friends to your room for theme parties or baby showers. Have a luau, celebrate holidays, decorate the room, and eat themed food. Yes, you are on bed rest, but you can laugh and have fun too!

66

Pregnancy Perseverance

My soul is in deep anguish. How long, Lord, how long?
—PSALM 6:3

*May the Lord direct your hearts into God's
love and Christ's perseverance.*
—2 THESSALONIANS 3:5

*And let us run with perseverance the race marked out for us,
fixing our eyes on Jesus, the pioneer and perfecter of faith.*
—HEBREWS 12:1-2

*Brothers and sisters, as an example of patience in the face of
suffering, take the prophets who spoke in the name of the Lord.
As you know, we count as blessed those who have persevered.
You have heard of Job's perseverance and have seen what the Lord
finally brought about. The Lord is full of compassion and mercy.*
—JAMES 5:10-11

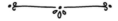

I was on bed rest for two months, and daily I thought, *Come
quickly, babies!* Some women are on bed rest for longer. It takes
perseverance to keep going and not lose your sanity. For some
women, bed rest is a long and boring time, and perseverance is

needed to keep going. For other women, bed rest isn't peaceful, but it's turmoil every day with complications, pain, worry, or sickness. Either way, the only thing you can do is persevere through it. God knows your trials and angst. He is helping you through—helping you persevere.

Why is perseverance a theme we often see in the Bible? It is because of sin. Because of sin, we are going to have trials. We are going to have bad or frustrating situations, through which we will have to persevere. God never promised easy lives, but He did promise He would be here with and for us. He promised our perseverance would be worth it in the end when Jesus comes again and we live with Him eternally.

Now when I look back at my time on bed rest ten years later, it seems like such a short time to persevere. Your perseverance on bed rest is but a short stint compared to the perseverance we must face awaiting Christ's return. We will face death, sadness, sickness, pain, rejection, and loneliness. It's inevitable in this sinful world. But take heart—God has overcome the world! Someday when we live eternally with God, our time of struggling on earth will seem so short. Lord, come quickly!

L I S T E N

"Hold on to Me" by Lauren Daigle
"The Comeback" by Danny Gokey
"We Are Brave" by Shawn McDonald

Bed Rest Survival Tip

———— ⁊ • ⁊ ————

Nothing takes perseverance like puzzles. Work on some jigsaw puzzles, brainteasers, crossword puzzles, or sudoku puzzles. It will feel good to accomplish something when you finish it.

67
Healing Hands

For he wounds, but he also binds up; he
injures, but his hands also heal.

—JOB 5:18

Praise the Lord, my soul, and forget not all his benefits—
who forgives all your sins and heals all your diseases.

—PSALM 103:2–3

There are different kinds of working, but in all of them
and in everyone it is the same God at work … Now to each
one the manifestation of the Spirit is given for the common
good. To one there is given through the Spirit the message of
wisdom … to another gifts of healing by that one Spirit.

—1 CORINTHIANS 12:6–8, 9

Have confidence in your leaders and submit to their
authority, because they keep watch over you as those who
must give an account. Do this so that their work will be a
joy, not a burden, for that would be of no benefit to you.

—HEBREWS 13:17

STACEY PYLMAN

Doctors are so smart. They have so much knowledge of science, diseases, the body, symptoms, and medicines, to name a few. So much of their job and knowledge is unknown to us as patients, but we trust that they know how to care for us and our families. When we are sick, wounded, or in pain, we look to our doctors to fix us. Sometimes our doctors are able to do so, and we rejoice. Sometimes they aren't. Even though they are very smart, they are still only human. They don't know the body like the Creator knows the body, but God works through their hands to heal many.

It isn't surprising that Jesus is referred to as the Great Physician. He spent a lot of time on earth healing the sick. He was able to do miraculous healing that doctors on earth could never do. He has control over sickness, disease, and sin. Jesus came to heal not only our bodies but also our hearts. He came to heal us from the disease of sin.

Often we are impatient, and we want the doctors to immediately fix us. Why do we have to suffer? Why can't they figure this out? We impatiently cry to God for healing. Sometimes God doesn't say yes to our request for earthly healing. Actually, our earthly bodies will never be fully healed. They are in a constant state of decay. But that isn't the end of the story. God has promised to heal us from all sin, sickness, and disease when we join Him in heaven in new bodies and live with Him eternally. Thank You, Great Physician!

L I S T E N

"Healing Rain" by Michael W. Smith
"Healer" by Kari Jobe
"Healing Is Here" by Deluge

Bed Rest Survival Tip

———❧•❧———

Write thank-you cards to your doctors today and deliver them before you leave the hospital. Your doctors have a very difficult job at times, and they have made sacrifices in their lives to care for the sick and suffering. They are truly a gift from God.

68

Struggling with Big Decisions

My son, if you accept my words and store up my commands
within you, turning your ear to wisdom and applying your heart
to understanding—indeed, if you call out for insight and cry
aloud for understanding, and if you look for it as for silver and
search for it as for hidden treasure, then you will understand the
fear of the Lord and find the knowledge of God. For the Lord gives
wisdom; from his mouth come knowledge and understanding.

—PROVERBS 2:1-6

I am the Lord your God, who teaches you what is best
for you, who directs you in the way you should go.

—ISAIAH 48:17

And pray in the Spirit on all occasions with
all kinds of prayers and requests.

—EPHESIANS 6:18

If any of you lacks wisdom, you should ask God, who gives
generously to all without finding fault, and it will be given
to you. But when you ask, you must believe and not doubt.

—JAMES 1:5-6

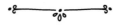

Of course, I had to make decisions in my life before I had kids. But for some reason, once I became a mom and had to make decisions that affected my children, the decisions seemed bigger and more difficult to make. When I was on bed rest, I had to decide whether I wanted to stay in the hospital or go home. I had to decide whether to enter a clinical trial study. Later when I was at home with preemies, I had to decide whether I should let visitors in my house. As my kids got older, the decisions didn't become easier. I told my friends and family, "I just wish God would send me an email and tell me what to do."

Sometimes we feel like it's a coin flip whether we make the right decision. Will we decide wrongly and see our families suffer? It feels like too much responsibility. The truth is, we never know the right decision without asking God what He wants us to do. God tells us in the Bible to seek wisdom and understanding from Him. We need to pray and ask for wisdom and apply the lessons in the Bible to our decision-making. Often God makes it clear to us what He desires by opening some doors and closing others. Sometimes God speaks through wise Christian brothers or sisters. Before making your big decisions, pray and ask God to show you what He wants.

L I S T E N

"Thy Word" by Amy Grant
"You Lead" by Jamie Grace
"Light It Up" by Terrian

Bed Rest Survival Tip

———— ❧•❧ ————

In your prayer journal, make a list of Christians from whom you could seek wise counsel when facing big decisions. Also, reflect on and write about times when God opened doors and closed doors to show you the way.

69

Let Me out of This Prison!

Truly I am your servant, Lord; I serve you just as my
mother did; you have freed me from my chains.

—PSALM 116:16

He upholds the cause of the oppressed and gives food
to the hungry. The Lord sets prisoners free.

—PSALM 146:7

Jesus replied, "Very truly I tell you, everyone who sins is a slave
to sin ... So if the Son sets you free, you will be free indeed."

—JOHN 8:34, 36

Now the Lord is the Spirit, and where the
Spirit of the Lord is, there is freedom.

—2 CORINTHIANS 3:17

Now I want you to know, brothers and sisters, that what has
happened to me has actually served to advance the gospel. As a
result, it has become clear throughout the whole palace guard and
to everyone else that I am in chains for Christ. And because of my
chains, most of the brothers and sisters have become confident in
the Lord and dare all the more to proclaim the gospel without fear.

PHILIPPIANS 1:12–14

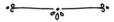

Are the walls closing in around you? Do you feel like you are in a prison cell? Do you want to yell, "Let me out"? These are all very normal feelings when you are on bed rest, confined to a room. The same walls day after day seem to be moving in, and the room is getting smaller. You yearn for freedom—freedom to go outside, to get in a car and drive, to travel, to explore!

For this season of your life, you are called to be still and remain in this room, just as Paul was called to sit in a prison cell for a season. Paul was in chains in a prison, and unlike you, he didn't even have a bed to sit in. But that didn't mean that God cared less about him or for him. Jesus was the only freedom Paul wanted, and He is the only freedom you need.

You may be confined to a room, but you have been given ultimate freedom from your sins through Christ! This freedom cannot be taken away, unlike your car keys. This freedom is eternal, and all you need to do is ask Jesus to be your Savior and choose to follow Him. Freedom in this world, although great, is only a taste of the freedom we experience in Christ. Our chains are gone; we've been set free!

L I S T E N

"Amazing Grace (My Chains Are Gone)" by Chris Tomlin
"Made to Fly" by Colton Dixon

Bed Rest Survival Tip

———— ❧•❧ ————

If you are doing bed rest in the hospital or at home, ask your doctor if you can have short wheelchair rides outside for fresh air. If not, don't forget to open the windows and let the fresh air inside.

70

Labor Pains

A woman giving birth to a child has pain because her time
has come; but when her baby is born she forgets the anguish
because of her joy that a child is born into the world. So it is
with you: Now is your time of grief, but I will see you again
and you will rejoice, and no one will take away your joy.

—JOHN 16:21-22

To this end I strenuously [labor], with all the
energy Christ so powerfully works in me.

—COLOSSIANS 1:29

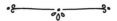

Some of you have gone through childbirth before, and you know
what is ahead. For others, this is the first time, and you don't
know what to expect. I was definitely scared of childbirth. I was a
first-time mom, and I didn't have any idea what to expect. When
I found out I was having triplets and a cesarean section was in
my future, I was actually relieved a little (my secret is out). It's so
silly. A cesarean section is a major surgery, and I should have been
more fearful of that than labor pain. However, I had done surgery
before, and I knew what to expect. I didn't know what to expect
when it came to natural childbirth. It's telling how so much of our
fear stems from the unknown.

Labor is painful. It's a result of sin, and God never wanted this kind of pain in the world. Nonetheless, here it is, and we need to endure it. But God doesn't leave sin to hurt us without turning it for His good. Your labor isn't in vain. He will bring good out of it.

In addition, God gives us strength to face our labor. He will be with you, holding your hand and giving you the power to do more than what you think your body can handle. He will also kindly help you forget the pain as you enjoy the results of your labor ... your new child.

When you pray today, ask God to give you peace and calm about the labor ahead. Ask Him to be there with you, holding your hand, and then trust that He will be.

L I S T E N

"Fear Not" by Chris Tomlin
"The Hurt and the Healer" by MercyMe

Bed Rest Survival Tip

Make plans for "birth day" if you haven't already. Decide who will be there with you and who will videotape or take photos or both. There are some photographers now who will take photos of the birth and first moments after birth. Decide whether this is something you would like and make plans. Make your list of people to call once the baby is born and write down their phone numbers too (chances are, you might not make all the calls).

71

Just Enough Light

In their hearts humans plan their course,
but the Lord establishes their steps.
—PROVERBS 16:9

She is clothed with strength and dignity;
she can laugh at the days to come.
—PROVERBS 31:25

I am the Lord your God, who teaches you what is best
for you, who directs you in the way you should go.
—ISAIAH 48:17

The Lord is good, a refuge in times of trouble.
He cares for those who trust in him.
—NAHUM 1:7

Jesus replied, "You do not realize now what I am
doing, but later you will understand."
—JOHN 13:7

I remember envying the mothers who had planned cesarean sections. They knew the day they were going to have their babies.

I'm such a planner and scheduler; I just wanted to know when my babies were going to come. I still struggle with unknown futures. When I was a stay-at-home mom with my girls, I was constantly wondering what I would do for a job when they went to school full-time. Now I worry about what life will be like when they all graduate and move out to college or elsewhere.

Fortunately for us, God created us to live only in the present. We don't know our futures because they would be too hard for our little brains to handle. We need to live out one day at a time and learn to trust that God holds our futures and the futures of our loved ones.

I love the poem "Just Enough Light" by Stormie Omartian. The words illustrate God's care for us by giving us just enough light for a step or two. If I had known in high school who I was going to marry, that I was going to have triplet daughters, and that I was going to get my doctorate, I would have been overwhelmed and tried to work ahead.

God reveals to us what we need to know only when we need to know it. Sometimes it's best if we don't plan. You might not know when your baby will come, if it will be a boy or girl, how many days your child will have on this earth, or how you are going to manage the future, but God knows. He has a plan, and it's perfect.

L I S T E N

"Trust" by Chris August
"The One Thing" by Paul Colman
"Thy Will" by Hillary Scott

Bed Rest Survival Tip

———— ཟ•ཟ ————

Find the poem "Just Enough Light" online and write it out on a card. Send it to other moms on bed rest or others in your life who are struggling with an unknown future. An excerpt of the poem is below.

Just Enough Light
by Stormie Omartian

Sometimes only the step I'm on,
Or the very next one ahead,
Is all that is illuminated for me.
God gives me just the amount of light I need
For the exact moment I need it.
At those times I walk in surrender
To faith, unable to see the future.

72

Struggling with Inner Conflict

Watch and pray so that you will not fall into temptation.
The spirit is willing, but the body is weak.

—MATTHEW 26:41

I do not understand what I do. For what I want to do I do not
do, but what I hate to do. And if I do what I do not want to do, I
agree that the law is good. As it is, it is no longer I myself who
do it, but it is sin living in me. For I know that good itself does
not dwell within me, that is, in my sinful nature. For I have
the desire to do what is good, but I cannot carry it out. For I do
not do the good I want to do; but the evil I do not want to do—
this I keep on doing. Now if I do what I do not want to do, it is
no longer I who do it, but it is sin living in me that does it.

—ROMANS 7:15–20

Why is it so hard to do the things that are right and good for us?
We are supposed to eat healthily, but we crave candy bars. We
know we should exercise, but we can talk ourselves into sitting on
the couch and watching a favorite TV show instead. We know we

should stay in bed and rest, but we just want to go to the kitchen and get something.

Yes, you face some inner conflict when lying on bed rest. You know you need to just lie there on your left side and drink water, but another part of you thinks, *I can get up and take care of something* or *I know I'm supposed to drink a lot of water, but I'm sick of it, and what does it really matter?* When I was on bed rest, I remember thinking, *Yes, I want the babies inside as long as possible, but I also just wish my water would break so this could be over!* I would joke with my nurses about doing jumping jacks in the bathroom so my water would break. I was tempted, but no, I didn't do it. Why in the world would I think about risking the life and health of my babies just to be done? Because it's hard. Because I just wanted to be done with pregnancy—I was uncomfortable.

This inner conflict we deal with reminds me of what Paul wrote about in Romans when he said, "For I do not do the good I want to do; but the evil I do not want to do—this I keep on doing." You see, we have a sin problem. We are born sinful, and because of this, we are often tempted to do what is wrong and think about only ourselves. I was thinking about myself and my comfort and then weighing that against the health of my babies. Some people would think that is crazy, and it is, but that's what a sinful mind can do. We do it all the time.

It's also crazy that we would ignore God's Word about the best ways to live and do things our own way instead—but we do so. When we struggle with inner conflict, the first thing we should do is pray—pray that we will listen to God's ways above our sinful nature. I didn't do jumping jacks in the bathroom to try to break my water because I was praying for these babies to be okay. I was praying that God would give me the strength to keep going. I was praying that I could put the babies' needs above my pain and suffering … and God answered.

L I S T E N

"Be Thou My Vision" by Selah

Bed Rest Survival Tip

Record your moving belly on video. This is something I forgot to do when I had the triplets inside me, and I wish I had a recording of how crazy my belly looked when they were all moving. It looked like they were wrestling in there. Now that's inner conflict! ;)

73

Finish Strong

The end of a matter is better than its beginning,
and patience is better than pride.

—ECCLESIASTES 7:8

Let us not become weary in doing good, for at the proper
time we will reap a harvest if we do not give up.

—GALATIANS 6:9

I have fought the good fight, I have finished
the race, I have kept the faith.

—2 TIMOTHY 4:7

Blessed is the one who perseveres under trial because,
having stood the test, that person will receive the crown of
life that the Lord has promised to those who love him.

—JAMES 1:12

There *is* something good about pregnancy bed rest … it has an end! It won't last forever. Remember when I said this was a marathon, not a sprint? Well, you are nearing the finish line now. You can see the light at the end of the tunnel. You have more bed rest days behind you than in front of you. You have accomplished a big feat, but that doesn't mean the rest of the days aren't going to be just as difficult, if not more. It's going to take everything you have in you to finish strong. Good thing God is in you.

The Holy Spirit is living inside you to give you patience, strength, and perseverance. Pray for the Holy Spirit to fight for you. Right now, when you are at your weakest, you can depend on God to use His strength. Don't give up now! You are almost there.

And when the day comes when your doctor tells you your bed rest has ended or when the baby makes its arrival, don't forget to thank God for bringing you the whole way. Well done, good and faithful servant.

L I S T E N

"Finish Strong" by Danny Gokey
"Finish Strong" by Jonathan Nelson

Bed Rest Survival Tip

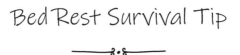

If you have other children who need a concrete representation of when you will be done with bed rest, together make a paper chain for the number of days you have left. Each day let them tear off one link in the chain.

74
Thankful during Trials

Because of your father's God, who helps you, because
of the Almighty, who blesses you with blessings
of the skies above, blessings of the deep springs
below, blessings of the breast and womb.
—GENESIS 49:25

Always giving thanks to God the Father for
everything, in the name of our Lord Jesus Christ.
—EPHESIANS 5:20

Let the peace of Christ rule in your hearts, since as members
of one body you were called to peace. And be thankful.
—COLOSSIANS 3:15

Rejoice always; pray continually; give thanks in all
circumstances, for this is God's will for you in Christ Jesus.
—1 THESSALONIANS 5:16-18

I'm telling you there is power in gratitude. I experienced this
myself years ago when I found myself depressed, frustrated with
my circumstances, and mad at the world. I thought I couldn't be
happy again and that I was stuck in a pit. But I wasn't stuck. Three

things got me out of that pit of sadness: God, therapy, and writing down three things I was thankful for each day.

After reading the book *One Thousand Gifts* by Ann Voskamp, I decided to write down three things I was thankful for every day for a year, as a prayer to God every morning. When a year passed, I continued for another year. Slowly, I was able to see the blessings in my life, and God brought me out of the pit of depression. There was something about focusing on the good things God had given me in my life instead of the bad that changed my outlook, my feelings, and eventually brought me out of depression into joy.

Possibly, you are facing some really depressing trials right now. You may have gotten bad news about your baby. You may be facing some bad financial circumstances. Your relationships might be stressed. How and why would God call us to be thankful in all circumstances? It's not that God is uncaring and wants us to thank Him when we are suffering because it makes *Him* happy. God knows that looking at what is good in our lives, at what He has provided for us, actually benefits us. It helps us to see God's care and provision in our lives; it helps us to be content and find joy.

If you are feeling depressed and unable to see any good in your life, I challenge you to find one to three things to be thankful for every day and write them down in your prayer journal. It might start with simple blessings like a bed, heat, air-conditioning, the sunrise, or a piece of chocolate. Then you will start to see the blessings of people in your life. Keep writing down what you are grateful for after the baby comes to help you see God's blessings in your life when you are exhausted. Try to do this for a year and see how your outlook on life changes.

L I  S T E N

"What Can I Do" by Paul Baloche
"Amen" by Micah Tyler

Bed Rest Survival Tip

Use this time before the baby to write thank-you cards to those who have given you gifts, made you meals, helped with your kids, or visited you.

75

Strength Will Rise as We Wait on the Lord

*The Lord gives strength to his people; the
Lord blesses his people with peace.*

—PSALM 29:11

*I lift my eyes up to the mountains— where does
my help come from? My help comes from the
Lord, the Maker of heaven and earth.*

—PSALM 121:1-2

*But those who hope in the Lord will renew their strength.
They will soar on wings like eagles; they will run and
not grow weary, they will walk and not be faint.*

—ISAIAH 40:31

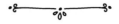

When you are on bed rest for a long time, your muscles become
weak, and your mental toughness can fizzle. You are just so done
with bed rest. You don't feel strong. However, there is no reason
for your spirit or soul to become weak. Your baby needs you to
be spiritually strong. We become spiritually strong when we talk

STACEY PYLMAN

with God, read the Bible, and pray. You will never have more time to do these things than when you are on bed rest.

It's strange to think that God promises that our strength will rise as we wait on Him. How can that be when we feel ourselves getting physically and mentally weaker? Remember, God's power is perfect in our weakness. As we wait on the Lord, we become spiritually stronger because we focus on Him and trust in Him. Also, God can use a strong spirit to make our minds and bodies strong as well.

Doing these daily devotions is helping you rise in strength as you wait on the Lord and wait for delivery day. Keep focusing on the Lord as your strength. He will give you strength for today, delivery day, and every day thereafter.

L I S T E N

"Everlasting God" by Chris Tomlin
"You Are My All in All/Canon in D
(Medley)" by the Gaither Vocal Band
"You Are My Strength" by Hillsong Worship

Bed Rest Survival Tip

When visitors ask you what they can bring, ask for fresh fruit. It's good for the body and soul. When someone brought me fresh-picked blueberries and strawberries, they were such a good gift. Really creative friends can make a fruit bouquet—it's more allergy friendly.

76
The Weight of It All

Cast your cares [burdens] on the Lord and he will sustain you; he will never let the righteous be shaken.
—PSALM 55:22

Praise be to the Lord, to God our Savior, who daily bears our burdens. Our God is a God who saves.
—PSALM 68:19-20

Come to me, all you who are weary and burdened, and I will give you rest. Take my yoke upon you and learn from me, for I am gentle and humble in heart, and you will find rest for your souls. For my yoke is easy and my burden is light.
—MATTHEW 11:28

Carry each other's burdens, and in this way you will fulfill the law of Christ.
—GALATIANS 6:2

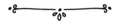

Weight. You probably don't even want to think about it. You may have to step on that scale from time to time, and it might be hard to look at the numbers. Even if you try to stay in denial about your increasing pregnancy weight, you know it exists. You can feel it.

You know the extra pounds are weighing you down, making it harder to move or get comfortable. But what a joy it is to float in the bathtub when you are pregnant! You feel weightless, and there is no pressure. You feel light and free.

Weight often has a negative connotation in our lives. We use phrases like "The weight of the world is on my shoulders" and "It is weighing on me." Weight like this is a stress, worry, or fear. The weight on us wears us down. It affects us mentally and physically. When we eventually feel relief, we say, "A weight has been lifted."

The Bible talks about these stressor weights as burdens. God tells us three things about burdens. First, we will have burdens in this world. We can choose the heavy burdens by following the world, or we can take the light burden of following Jesus. Second, God will take some burdens from us. The Bible says to cast our burdens on Him, and He will bear them for us. Third, God asks us to carry each other's burdens to lighten the load. If someone asked you if he or she could carry the weight of your pregnancy for a while, wouldn't you let him or her so you could have a break? Maybe that's not physically possible, but you can ask God to take away or ease your burdens, and you can ask friends and family to lift some stress burdens from your shoulders.

L I S T E N

"Burdens" by Jamie Kimmett
"Cast Your Burden" by Gateway Worship

Bed Rest Survival Tip

———— 8·8 ————

Ask someone to draw you a bath often. Floating weightlessly in the warm water with music playing can do wonders for aches and pains.

77

The Pain of Childbirth

To the woman he said, "I will make your pains in childbearing
very severe; with painful labor you will give birth to children."

—GENESIS 3:16

But as for me, afflicted and in pain—may your
salvation, God, protect me. I will praise God's name
in song and glorify him with thanksgiving.

—PSALM 69:29-30

I consider that our present sufferings are not worth
comparing with the glory that will be revealed in us.

—ROMANS 8:18

To this end I strenuously contend, with all the
energy Christ so powerfully works in me.

—COLOSSIANS 1:29

But if you suffer for doing good and you endure
it, this is commendable before God. To this you were
called, because Christ suffered for you, leaving you
an example, that you should follow in his steps.

—1 PETER 2:20-21

He will wipe every tear from their eyes. There will
be no more death or mourning or crying or pain,
for the old order of things has passed away.
—REVELATION 21:4

Toward the end of the pregnancy, pains tend to increase, and the days get harder. Your back hurts more, your hips ache more, your reflux may be worse, and there might not be a lot of room for your baby, who is pushing on parts of you that cause pain. Pain is inevitable with pregnancy and labor. When Eve brought sin into the world, the consequence was pain with childbirth. Even with the best drugs, there will be pain involved with carrying and delivering a baby. In this sinful world, we will have pain, and God knows our pain.

Still, we can endure because God gives us strength to endure, and our endurance through pain and suffering for good is commendable before God. Bringing life into this world is so good, and God's glory will be seen in and through this child. Your labor is for the Creator's glory, and He will see you through.

Our pain and suffering here on earth are but labor pains before Christ comes. As we get closer to Christ's return, sin will get worse, and suffering will increase. We will groan for His return. But just as our labor pains will end and we will be blessed with a new baby life to celebrate, we also have hope that the pain in this world won't endure forever. There will be an end to all pain and suffering when Christ comes again, and we will celebrate our new lives. What a glorious day that will be!

L I S T E N

"There Will Be a Day" by Jeremy Camp
"Soon and Very Soon" by Selah

Bed Rest Survival Tip

———— 𝄞•𝄢 ————

Make sure to be honest about your pain and communicate it to your doctors and nurses. They will give you ways to alleviate some pain that is safe for you and the baby. Also ask for heat or massages for sore muscles.

Be Still Christian Song List

Alphabetical by Title

"A Mother's Prayer" by Keith & Kristyn Getty
"Abide with Me" by Audrey Assad
"All I Need Is You" by Lecrae
"Almost Home" by MercyMe
"Amazing Grace (My Chains Are Gone)" by Chris Tomlin
"Amen" by Micah Tyler
"Be Still My Soul" by Kari Jobe
"Be Still" by Hillsong Live
"Be Thou My Vision" by Selah
"Be Unto Your Name/Holy, Holy, Holy" by Brian Doerksen
"Beautiful" by Bethany Dillon
"Before the Morning" by Josh Wilson
"Behold Our God" by Sovereign Grace Music
"Better than a Hallelujah" by Amy Grant
"Breathe" by Jonny Diaz
"Broken Hallelujah" by Mandisa
"Broken Hallelujah" by The Afters
"Brother" by NEEDTOBREATHE
"Burdens" by Jamie Kimmett
"Cast Your Burden" by Gateway Worship
"Center of It" by Chris August
"Children of God" by Third Day
"Come Jesus Come" by Stephen McWhirter

"Cry Out to Jesus" by Third Day
"Deep in Love With You" by Michael W. Smith
"Do Everything" by Steven Curtis Chapman
"Do Not Worry" by Ellie Holcomb
"Drops in the Ocean" by Hawk Nelson
"Even If" by MercyMe
"Even When It Hurts" by Hillsong UNITED
"Everlasting God" by Chris Tomlin
"Every Bit of Lovely" by Jamie Grace
"Every Season" by Nichole Nordeman
"Eye of the Storm" by Ryan Stevenson
"Family of God" by Newsboys
"Fear Is a Liar" by Zach Williams
"Fear Not" by Chris Tomlin
"Find You Here" by Ellie Holcomb
"Finish Strong" by Danny Gokey
"Finish Strong" by Jonathan Nelson
"For the Good" by Riley Clemmons
"For This Child" by Ken Blount
"Friend Medley" by Anthem Lights
"Go Down Singing" by Tim Be Told
"God Gave Me You" by Dave Barnes
"God Hears" by Newsong
"God Is Good" by Jon McReynolds
"God of My Everything" by Bebo Norman
"God Only Knows" by for KING & COUNTRY and Dolly Parton
"God So Loved" by We The Kingdom
"God Who Listens" by Chris Tomlin
"Gold" by Britt Nicole
"Good Feeling" by Austin French
"Good Morning" by Mandisa (featuring TobyMac)
"Great Is Thy Faithfulness" by Fernando Ortega
"He Knows My Name" by Francesca Battistelli
"He Knows My Name" by Paul Baloche

"He Knows" by Jeremy Camp
"He Still Does (Miracles)" by Hawk Nelson
"Healer" by Kari Jobe
"Healing Is Here" by Deluge
"Healing Rain" by Michael W. Smith
"Hear My Prayer" by E. Dewey Smith, Jr. & the Hope Mass Choir
"Hold Me Jesus" by Rich Mullins
"Hold on to Me" by Lauren Daigle
"Home" by Chris Tomlin
"How Great Thou Art" by Carrie Underwood and Vince Gill
"Human Condition" by Unspoken
"Human" by Holly Starr (featuring Matthew Parker)
"Hunger" by CeCe Winans
"Hungry (Falling on My Knees)" by Vineyard Worship (featuring
    Kathryn Scott)
"I Am Weak" by Craig Aven
"I Shall Not Want" by Audrey Assad
"I Smile" by Kirk Franklin
"I Surrender All" by Carrie Underwood
"I Will Be Here" by Steven Curtis Chapman
"I Will Carry You" by Michael W. Smith
"I Will Fear No More" by The Afters
"I Will Rest in You" by Jaci Velasquez
"If We Are the Body" by Casting Crowns
"Image of God" by We Are Messengers
"It Is Well with My Soul" by Audrey Assad or Anthem Lights
"It Is Well" by Bethel Music and Kristene DiMarco
"Jesus Is Coming Back" by Jordan Feliz
"Jesus Loves Me" by Christy Nockels
"Joy Comes in the Morning" by Baylor Wilson
"Keep Me in the Moment" by Jeremy Camp
"Laugh Out Loud" by Jason Gray
"Laughter Just like a Medicine" by BeBe Winans
"Lift Me Up" by The Afters

"Light It Up" by Terrian
"Lights Shine Bright" by TobyMac
"Living Hope" by Phil Wickham
"Living Sacrifice (Live)" by Brandon Lake
"Living Waters" by Keith & Kristyn Getty
"Look Up Child" by Lauren Daigle
"Lord I Believe in You" by Crystal Lewis
"Lord, I Need You" by Matt Maher
"Love Never Fails" by Brandon Heath
"Made to Fly" by Colton Dixon
"Miracles" by Colton Dixon
"Never Alone" by BarlowGirl
"Never Let You Down" Hawk Nelson
"New Today" by Micah Tyler
"No Impossible with You" by I Am They
"Oh How I Love You" by Zacardi Cortez
"Oh My Soul" by Casting Crowns
"Oh, the Deep, Deep Love of Jesus" by Audrey Assad
"On My Knees" by Jaci Valesquez or Nicole C. Mullen
"One Heartbeat at a Time" by Steven Curtis Chapman
"Only Jesus" by Brian Johnson
"Our Hope Endures" by Natalie Grant
"Overcomer" by Mandisa
"Patient" by Apollo LTD
"Peace Be Still" by Hope Darst
"Power of Prayer" by Matthew West
"Power" by Elevation Worship
"Reach" by Peter Furler
"Reason" by Unspoken
"Remember Me" by Mark Schultz
"Rescue" by Lauren Daigle
"Restless" by Audrey Assad
"River of Life" by Mac Powell
"Run On" by Kara Coats (featuring Allie Ray)

"Run the Race" by Holly Starr
"Running" by Hillsong (Live)
"Savior, like a Shepherd Lead Us" by Fernando Ortega
"Scars" by I Am They
"Scars" by TobyMac
"Seasons" by Hillsong Worship
"See the Light" by TobyMac
"Shepherd" by Crowder
"Shine a Light" by Elevation Worship
"Shoulders" by for KING & COUNTRY
"Simple Gifts (Live)" by Jim Brickman
"Situation" by Jon McReynolds
"Sky Spills Over" by Michael W. Smith
"Slow Down" by Nichole Nordeman
"Soon and Very Soon" by Selah
"Sparrow" by Audrey Assad
"Sparrows" by Jason Gray
"Stand in Faith" by Danny Gokey
"Stay and Wait" by Hillsong UNITED
"Stronger" by Mandisa
"Strong Enough" by Matthew West
"Take My Hand" by Shawn McDonald
"The Benediction" by Timothy James Meaney
"The Blessing" by Kari Jobe and Cody Carnes
"The Comeback" by Danny Gokey
"The Giving" by Michael W. Smith
"The Hurt and the Healer" by MercyMe
"The One Thing" by Paul Colman
"The Prayer" by Andrea Bocelli and Celine Dion
"The Proof of Your Love" by for KING & COUNTRY
"There Is Power" by Lincoln Brewster
"There Was Jesus" by Zach Williams and Dolly Parton
"There Will Be a Day" by Jeremy Camp
"Thrive" by Casting Crowns

"Thy Will" by Hillary Scott

"Thy Word" by Amy Grant

"Trading My Sorrows" by Darrell Evans

"Trust in You" by Lauren Daigle

"Trust" by Chris August

"Truth Be Told" by Matthew West

"Truth I'm Standing On" by Leanna Crawford

"Watch over Me" by Aaron Shust

"Waymaker" by Mandisa

"We Believe" by Newsboys

"What Can I Do" by Paul Baloche

"When We Pray" by Tauren Wells

"While I'm Waiting" by John Williams

"Who Am I" by Point of Grace

"Yes He Can" by CAIN

"Yes I Will" by Vertical Worship

"Masterpiece" by Sandi Patty

"You Are My All in All/Canon in D (Medley)" by the Gaither Vocal Band

"You Are My Hope" by Skillet

"You Are My Strength" by Hillsong Worship

"You Know My Name" by Tasha Cobbs Leonard (featuring Jimi Cravity)

"You Lead" by Jamie Grace

"You're Not Alone" by Meredith Andrews

"Your Hands" by JJ Heller

"Your Plans for Us" by Eleventh Hour Worship

"Your Wings" by Lauren Daigle

By Topic

Children of God
"Beautiful" by Bethany Dillon
"Children of God" by Third Day
"Every Bit of Lovely" by Jamie Grace
"Family of God" by Newsboys
"Gold" by Britt Nicole
"He Knows My Name" by Francesca Battistelli
"He Knows My Name" by Paul Baloche
"Image of God" by We Are Messengers
"Remember Me" by Mark Schultz
"The Blessing" by Kari Jobe and Cody Carnes
"You Know My Name" by Tasha Cobbs Leonard (featuring Jimi Cravity)

Contentment
"All I Need Is You" by Lecrae
"God Is Good" by Jon McReynolds
"Hunger" by CeCe Winans
"Hungry (Falling on My Knees)" by Vineyard Worship (featuring Kathryn Scott)
"I Shall Not Want" by Audrey Assad
"Only Jesus" by Brian Johnson
"Reason" by Unspoken
"Situation" by Jon McReynolds

Encouragement, Comfort, and Protection
"Abide with Me" by Audrey Assad
"Almost Home" by MercyMe
"Brother" by NEEDTOBREATHE
"Center of It" by Chris August
"For the Good" by Riley Clemmons

"Friend Medley" by Anthem Lights
"Go Down Singing" by Tim Be Told
"God Is Good" by Jon McReynolds
"God Only Knows" by for KING & COUNTRY and Dolly Parton
"He Knows" by Jeremy Camp
"Home" by Chris Tomlin
"I Smile" by Kirk Franklin
"I Will Carry You" by Michael W. Smith
"It Is Well" by Bethel Music and Kristene DiMarco
"Laugh Out Loud" by Jason Gray
"Laughter Just like a Medicine" by BeBe Winans
"Lift Me Up" by The Afters
"Look Up Child" by Lauren Daigle
"Made to Fly" by Colton Dixon
"Never Let You Down" Hawk Nelson
"New Today" by Micah Tyler
"Overcomer" by Mandisa
"Reach" by Peter Furler
"Take My Hand" by Shawn McDonald
"The Blessing" by Kari Jobe and Cody Carnes
"The Comeback" by Danny Gokey
"There Was Jesus" by Zach Williams and Dolly Parton
"Thrive" by Casting Crowns
"Your Hands" by JJ Heller
"Your Wings" by Lauren Daigle

Hope, Trust, and Fear
"Before the Morning" by Josh Wilson
"Eye of the Storm" by Ryan Stevenson
"Fear Is a Liar" by Zach Williams
"Fear Not" by Chris Tomlin
"Hold Me Jesus" by Rich Mullins
"I Will Fear No More" by The Afters
"It Is Well with My Soul" by Audrey Assad or Anthem Lights

"Living Hope" by Phil Wickham
"Made to Fly" by Colton Dixon
"Oh My Soul" by Casting Crowns
"Our Hope Endures" by Natalie Grant
"Shoulders" by for KING & COUNTRY
"The One Thing" by Paul Colman
"Thy Will" by Hillary Scott
"Trust in You" by Lauren Daigle
"Trust" by Chris August
"Truth I'm Standing On" by Leanna Crawford
"We Are Brave" by Shawn McDonald
"You Are My Hope" by Skillet

Faith

"Even If" by MercyMe
"Even When It Hurts" by Hillsong UNITED
"For the Good" by Riley Clemmons
"Lord I Believe in You" by Crystal Lewis
"Stand in Faith" by Danny Gokey
"We Believe" by Newsboys

Gratitude

"Amen" by Micah Tyler
"Great Is Thy Faithfulness" by Fernando Ortega
"Keep Me in the Moment" by Jeremy Camp
"What Can I Do" by Paul Baloche
"Who Am I" by Point of Grace

Guidance

"Be Thou My Vision" by Selah
"Savior, like a Shepherd Lead Us" by Fernando Ortega
"Shepherd" by Crowder
"Thy Word" by Amy Grant
"You Lead" by Jamie Grace

"Your Plans for Us" by Eleventh Hour Worship
"Watch over Me" by Aaron Shust

Humility
"Human Condition" by Unspoken
"Human" by Holly Starr (featuring Matthew Parker)
"Truth Be Told" by Matthew West

Light
"Light It Up" by Terrian
"Lights Shine Bright" by TobyMac
"See the Light" by TobyMac
"Shine a Light" by Elevation Worship

Lonely
"Brother" by NEEDTOBREATHE
"Find You Here" by Ellie Holcomb
"Friend Medley" by Anthem Lights
"I Will Be Here" by Steven Curtis Chapman
"Never Alone" by BarlowGirl
"Reach" by Peter Furler
"Take My Hand" by Shawn McDonald
"You're Not Alone" by Meredith Andrews

Love
"Deep in Love With You" by Michael W. Smith
"Drops in the Ocean" by Hawk Nelson
"God Gave Me You" by Dave Barnes
"God So Loved" by We The Kingdom
"I Will Be Here" by Steven Curtis Chapman
"Jesus Loves Me" by Christy Nockels
"Living Sacrifice (Live)" by Brandon Lake
"Living Waters" by Keith & Kristyn Getty
"Love Never Fails" by Brandon Heath

"Oh How I Love You" by Zacardi Cortez
"Oh, the Deep, Deep Love of Jesus" by Audrey Assad
"The Proof of Your Love" by for KING & COUNTRY
"Masterpiece" by Sandi Patty

Miracles/Power
"He Still Does (Miracles)" by Hawk Nelson
"Miracles" by Colton Dixon
"No Impossible with You" by I Am They
"Power" by Elevation Worship
"There Is Power" by Lincoln Brewster
"Waymaker" by Mandisa
"Yes He Can" by CAIN

Mothering
"A Mother's Prayer" by Keith & Kristyn Getty
"Do Everything" by Steven Curtis Chapman
"For This Child" by Ken Blount
"One Heartbeat at a Time" by Steven Curtis Chapman

Overwhelmed, Stressed, or Sad
"Breathe" by Jonny Diaz
"Broken Hallelujah" by Mandisa
"Broken Hallelujah" by The Afters
"Burdens" by Jamie Kimmett
"Cast Your Burden" by Gateway Worship
"Hold on to Me" by Lauren Daigle
"Joy Comes in the Morning" by Baylor Wilson
"I Surrender All" by Carrie Underwood
"Lord, I Need You" by Matt Maher
"Rescue" by Lauren Daigle

Patience
"Be Still My Soul" by Kari Jobe

"Be Still" by Hillsong Live
"Come Jesus Come" by Stephen McWhirter
"Everlasting God" by Chris Tomlin
"Every Season" by Nichole Nordeman
"I Will Rest in You" by Jaci Velasquez
"Jesus Is Coming Back" by Jordan Feliz
"Patient" by Apollo LTD
"Peace Be Still" by Hope Darst
"Restless" by Audrey Assad
"Seasons" by Hillsong Worship
"Soon and Very Soon" by Selah
"Stay and Wait" by Hillsong UNITED
"There Will Be a Day" by Jeremy Camp
"While I'm Waiting" by John Williams

Praise
"Amazing Grace (My Chains Are Gone)" by Chris Tomlin
"Amen" by Micah Tyler
"Be Unto Your Name/Holy, Holy, Holy" by Brian Doerksen
"Behold Our God" by Sovereign Grace Music
"How Great Thou Art" by Carrie Underwood and Vince Gill
"Sky Spills Over" by Michael W. Smith
"Yes I Will" by Vertical Worship

Prayer
"God Hears" by Newsong
"God Who Listens" by Chris Tomlin
"Hear My Prayer" by E. Dewey Smith, Jr. & the Hope Mass Choir
"On My Knees" by Jaci Valesquez or Nicole C. Mullen
"Power of Prayer" by Matthew West
"The Prayer" by Andrea Bocelli and Celine Dion
"When We Pray" by Tauren Wells

Sickness or Hurt
"Better than a Hallelujah" by Amy Grant
"Cry Out to Jesus" by Third Day
"God of My Everything" by Bebo Norman
"Healer" by Kari Jobe
"Healing Is Here" by Deluge
"Healing Rain" by Michael W. Smith
"Scars" by I Am They
"Scars" by TobyMac
"The Hurt and the Healer" by MercyMe
"Trading My Sorrows" by Darrell Evans

Weakness, Strength, or Perseverance
"Everlasting God" by Chris Tomlin
"Finish Strong" by Danny Gokey
"Finish Strong" by Jonathan Nelson
"I Am Weak" by Craig Aven
"Lord, I Need You" by Matt Maher
"Overcomer" by Mandisa
"Run On" by Kara Coats (featuring Allie Ray)
"Run the Race" by Holly Starr
"Running" by Hillsong (Live)
"Stronger" by Mandisa
"Strong Enough" by Matthew West
"The Comeback" by Danny Gokey
"You Are My All in All/Canon in D (Medley)" by the Gaither
    Vocal Band
"You Are My Strength" by Hillsong Worship

Worry
"Do Not Worry" by Ellie Holcomb
"Oh My Soul" by Casting Crowns
"Sparrow" by Audrey Assad
"Sparrows" by Jason Gray

Printed in the United States
by Baker & Taylor Publisher Services